Stefan Buczacki

Best
Pruning

Special Photography Howard Rice

HAMLYN

Publishing Director Laura Bamford
Creative Director Keith Martin
Design Manager Bryan Dunn
Designer TT Designs
Executive Editor Julian Brown
Editor Karen O'Grady
Production Julie Hadingham
Picture Research Sally Claxton, Liz Fowler
Researcher Hilary Engel
Special Photography Howard Rice

First published in Great Britain in 1998
by Hamlyn
an imprint of Reed Consumer Books Limited
Michelin House, 81 Fulham Road,
London SW3 6RB
and Auckland, Melbourne, Singapore and Toronto

© Reed Consumer Books Limited 1998
Text © Stefan Buczacki 1998
Design © Reed Consumer Books Limited 1998

Produced by Toppan
Printed in China

A catalogue record for this book is available from
the British Library

ISBN 0 600 590 224

CONTENTS

Introduction 4

Terminology of Pruning 6

Tools 8

Restorative Pruning 10

Pruning for Ornamental Effect 12

Pruning for Damage and Disease Control 14

The Timing of Pruning 16

General Pruning Techniques 18

Pruning and Flowering time 20

Pruning and Flowering Time/Stooling 22

Techniques with Trees 24

Climbers 26

Specialised Fruit Pruning 28

Trees, Shrubs and Climbers 30

Roses 56

Hedges 62

Topiary 66

Soft Fruit 70

Acid Soil Fruits 74

Tree Fruit 75

Climbing Fruit 90

Herbaceous Plants 92

Index 94

INTRODUCTION

ABOVE: **Left to its own devices, a climbing plant like this rose 'Golden Showers' will flower at the top only**

BELOW: **By a combination of pruning and training the shoots horizontally, this 'Dublin Bay' rose has been encouraged to cover the wall**

Everyone has heard of pruning. All gardeners do it at some time or another, and yet there's no denying that it's one of the less immediately accessible gardening skills. It is a technique from which many gardeners shy away, and even those who practise it routinely are often blissfully unaware of the reasoning behind their actions, or even that such reasoning actually exists. This is unfortunate, first because pruning is neither complicated nor illogical, second because it can be immensely satisfying, and third because, done properly, it may make the difference between having plants that are rewarding and efficient and those that truly are neither use nor ornament.

While pruning is generally thought to be an operation performed only on trees and shrubs, any removal of shoots, branches, flowers or other parts from a growing plant is a type of pruning and subject, therefore, to the same underlying principles. The regular pruning of a young plant will dictate its overall shape as it matures, an operation called training. As well as producing a plant of convenient form for a particular site in the garden, the choice of training method can have a considerable influence on the plant's effectiveness and productivity. Cordon or fan-trained fruit trees grown against walls are good examples of this (page 28).

Training a plant into a chosen shape is, therefore, the first objective of pruning. The second is to increase the production of leafy shoots (part of the reason for pruning or clipping hedges), or flowers and fruits (the usual reason with ornamental and fruit plants). A third purpose of pruning is to encourage overall vigorous growth by allowing light and air to reach all parts of the plant through the removal of overcrowded shoots and branches. Fourth and finally, pruning can be used to improve the health of a plant by removing either diseased parts or those redundant or

moribund tissues (dead flowers, for instance) that are likely to provide a foothold for disease-causing fungi and bacteria. Regular deadheading of roses and of summer-flowering herbaceous and bedding plants, therefore, is important for both aesthetic and practical reasons.

Pruning does not dictate the shape, form and productivity of a plant solely through the removal of certain shoots.

Shaping is achieved more specifically because taking off the end of a shoot, with its associated buds, actually stimulates buds lower down the shoot to start into active growth. This is why regularly clipping a hedge will thicken its overall growth. A similar effect can be achieved by bending a shoot downwards towards the horizontal, rather than cutting it off, a technique especially valuable when the lower parts of a wall are to be clothed with a climbing rose, or when some fruit trees are producing long shoots but few accessible fruit. This important effect is achieved, in both cases, by disrupting the phenomenon called apical dominance, in which the growing buds at and close to the tip (apex) of a shoot produce chemicals that inhibit the growth of those below them.

Over the next few pages, I've elaborated on some of the techniques of pruning and have suggested the essential tools that you will need to do the job properly.

The results of attention to pruning are clearly evident in a garden of healthy, attractive plants

*P*runing uses rather more jargon than most other areas of gardening, with the possible exception of propagation. Although a number of terms are unique to the subject, it also draws on more everyday phrases and expressions that can mean different things to different gardeners. To one person, a weak shoot is one that is thin; to another, it's one that is both long and thin; to yet another it's one of any thickness but unable to support the weight of fruit. As I am anxious that this book should be as free as possible from ambiguity and as I'm even more anxious that you should only cut off the parts of your plants that I intend, I have defined here some of the more frequently used expressions over which there might be confusion.

SALIENT FEATURES OF A PLANT

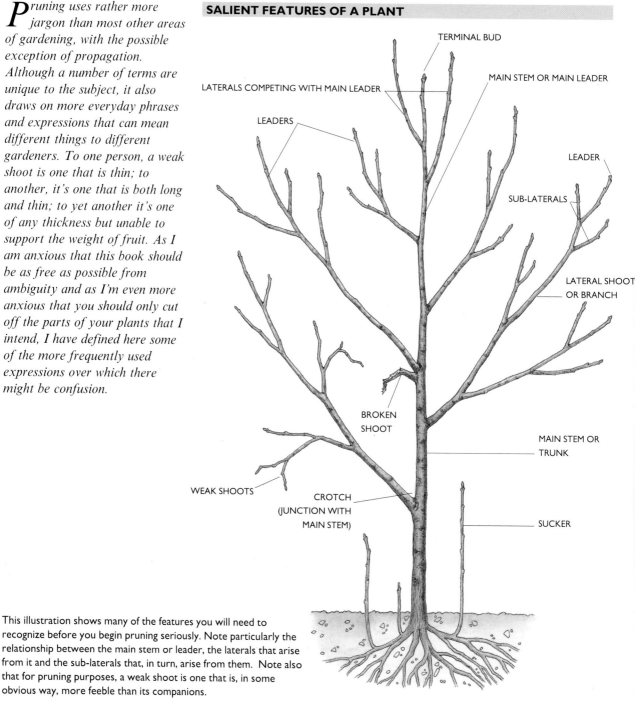

TERMINAL BUD

MAIN STEM OR MAIN LEADER

LATERALS COMPETING WITH MAIN LEADER

LEADERS

LEADER

SUB-LATERALS

LATERAL SHOOT OR BRANCH

BROKEN SHOOT

MAIN STEM OR TRUNK

WEAK SHOOTS

CROTCH (JUNCTION WITH MAIN STEM)

SUCKER

This illustration shows many of the features you will need to recognize before you begin pruning seriously. Note particularly the relationship between the main stem or leader, the laterals that arise from it and the sub-laterals that, in turn, arise from them. Note also that for pruning purposes, a weak shoot is one that is, in some obvious way, more feeble than its companions.

WEAK AND STRONG BUDS AND ANNUAL GROWTH

With many shrubs and trees, especially fruit trees, it's important to distinguish between weak and strong buds and to recognise the age of different parts of a shoot.

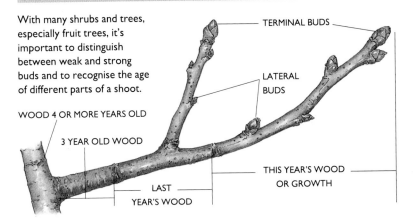

TERMINAL BUDS

LATERAL BUDS

WOOD 4 OR MORE YEARS OLD

3 YEAR OLD WOOD

LAST YEAR'S WOOD

THIS YEAR'S WOOD OR GROWTH

RECOGNISING A SPUR

FLOWERING/FRUITING SPUR

A spur is a short, stubby shoot on which flower/fruit buds develop.

CROWDED AND OPEN CENTRES

Crowded Here there is a mass of twiggy shoots, some dead or diseased, that have grown very close together. Many of them are touching and you can barely see daylight through the middle.

Open Here, you can see more daylight than plant. No shoots are touching and light and air can reach all of them equally. Dead or diseased shoots have been removed.

TOOLS

Using sharp secateurs will avoid damage to plant tissues

Although finger and thumb are valuable tools for pinching out soft shoot tips or the branches of non-woody plants, something more robust is necessary for most pruning tasks. Somewhere, in some form, all pruning tools have a cutting edge and the efficiency, sharpness and durability of this edge is the key to their success. A good cutting edge is costly to produce and I feel that buying the best quality is more important with pruning tools than with any other gardening tool.

Pruning with a knife is a very difficult and potentially amputational technique and I don't recommend it. So the most important pruning tool for normal garden use is a pair of secateurs or pruners (the two names are interchangeable). They fall into two basic patterns. The scissor or by-pass secateur has two blades cutting against each other, like a pair of scissors.

It has therefore, a slicing action that is very gentle on soft stems and gives a beautifully clean cut surface. The two blades are carefully aligned at the factory but can be damaged if they are used on very hard woody stems. The other type of secateur is based on an anvil pattern. It is a chopping tool with a single blade that cuts on to a flattened surface. Anvil secateurs are more robust and they can easily cut through very hard stems without being damaged. Admittedly a soft shoot can be crushed but I believe this is less of a threat than the possibility of damaging the tool itself if a by-pass secateur is misused. I urge serious gardeners to have a pair of both types, but I recommend the anvil pattern for the beginner or inexperienced gardener. As well as the two basic patterns, most manufacturers produce secateurs of

differing sizes and you should always check the maximum thickness of stem for which any size of secateurs is intended and don't use them on material thicker than this.

If you have large branches to cut, you will certainly need something more powerful; you require a pair of loppers. Traditional loppers work on the same principle as secateurs (usually of anvil pattern), and are available in versions with different handle lengths. Longer handles offer more reach into trees and large shrubs, while, of course, providing you with more leverage. Lever-action loppers provide the ultimate in cutting efficiency combined with ease of use and reach (page 12). You may, however, have even larger branches to cut. For branches of moderate thickness you need a curved pruning saw. Unlike a conventional saw, it is shaped so that it can be inserted between and among the branches of a tree or shrub without causing damage. For thicker branches, use a bow-saw.

For very small, or at least for non-woody plants, there is a further range of

A small toothed saw is needed for the neat removal of tree branches

cutting tools. Bushy plants, either those with fairly tough stems such as heathers, or softer tissued annuals can be trimmed back with hand shears. The conventional two-handed pattern is excellent but you will then be faced with the need to brush up all of the prunings. A single-handed shear conveniently overcomes these problems, enabling you to grasp the clump with one hand while the other operates the tool.

If you have tall trees that will need regular pruning, long-handled or even pole pruners and a pole saw will be needed. For most gardeners, however, this is an infrequent requirement and these tools are best hired when needed. Many gardeners with substantial tree lopping to undertake are tempted to buy a chain-saw. These are astonishingly efficient appliances in experienced hands, but they are also potentially the most dangerous of all gardening tools. The total removal of unwanted trees is also generally a matter for a professional. Apart from the difficulty and danger of felling the tree itself, there is no simple method of removing stumps. They must be dug up, ground down or winched out, the latter two especially being operations that require large and expensive equipment for which ready access must be available. I do strongly recommend that all substantial work on large trees be left to professionals.

Hand shears are the traditional tools to use for hedge cutting and should be used for small hedges or topiary. Modern powered hedge trimmers are, however, light, easy to use and safe, and give a very good finish with practice. But do stop regularly to look at your work and your line of cut; years of careful training and shaping can be undone in a moment's lack of concentration.

The production of suckers (shoots arising directly from the roots rather than the main stem or trunk) is a common problem with many garden trees and shrubs, especially where the chosen variety has been grafted on to a different rootstock. Suckers should always be removed for they will invariably draw nutrient away from the grafted variety but here, human power is best. They should be pulled, not cut away if the result isn't merely to be the stimulation of yet more suckers. But do wear very thick gloves, as even smooth looking stems can result in unpleasant abrasions.

Sometimes, brute strength is the best solution. Suckers are less likely to re-grow if they are torn out

RESTORATIVE PRUNING

No matter how good our intentions, none of use can find all of the time needed to give the correct care and attention to every plant every season. And we shall all very probably, at some stage, find ourselves the owners of plants that have, for some reason, been neglected. They may appear to be little more than tangled masses of moribund and probably diseased vegetation, but they may, nonetheless, be important structural features of the garden that have taken many years to reach their full size or they may be of choice or expensive varieties. Pruning can be their salvation, and takes on a remedial role, with the plants being rejuvenated through the careful removal of the older parts and retention of the more vigorous. Remember, too, that old and neglected

hedges can also very often be restored, either by hard pruning or by laying and I have given some guidance on this on page 62.

I must be honest and say that there are no hard and fast rules that you can follow in deciding whether a plant can or can't be salvaged. My advice would always be that if a plant is important by virtue of its size or other feature, it's always worth spending 12 months seeing what can be done. Old fruit trees are rather special cases, and as I suggest on page 80, your best plan with old apple or pear trees is that, provided they aren't heavily cankered, to leave them untouched, apart from the removal of dead branches. Forget about trying to bring them into cropping and accept them simply as aesthetic features. Old and unfruitful plum

trees are very likely to be harbouring silver leaf disease however and are best removed professionally.

Much of restorative pruning is common sense. The three main considerations are to remove dead or diseased parts, to remove branches that are crossing, rubbing or tangled, and to improve the overall shape, either for purely aesthetic reasons or because the plant has become an inconvenience, for example by draping itself across a path or against a window. But don't try to resurrect any overgrown tree or shrub in one operation. Spread the task over time. Do about one-third of the work in the first operation; wait 12 months and if things improve, continue in two more stages. If things are no better or indeed are worse, don't persevere.

The crown of this ash tree contains crossing and dead branches, only really evident in winter

Skillful thinning of the crown has removed the imperfect branches and admitted more light and air to the remainder

Never completely cut down an ailing plant in one operation, even if, like *Leycesteria formosa*, it is one that should routinely be pruned in this way. A healthy plant can cope with very hard pruning; a sick one generally can't, so always leave some shoots unpruned to enable the plant to draw water and nutrients from its roots. Professional gardeners refer to these shoots as 'sap-drawers'.

And do bear in mind that pruning alone won't necessarily improve a tree or shrub. The source of the problem may be unsuitable soil, incorrect planting, competition from grass or other vegetation, bad drainage or any of a number of other factors. Corrective pruning will often have to be combined with attention to one or more of these problems.

Some pruning books dwell at length on a technique called root pruning. I must say that in my gardening life, it is something that I have had to do rarely and don't think it is part of the everyday gardener's stock in trade. There are however a few occasions when it may play a part in a restorative pruning operation; not with trees or shrubs that are growing feebly, but with those that are growing too vigorously. Root pruning is most commonly used with apple, pear or a few types of ornamental trees but should never be done on plums or other *Prunus* species, willows or poplars as they will respond by excessive production of suckers. Root pruning is achieved by carefully digging a circular trench in autumn approximately 45cm (18in) deep and at a radius from the trunk determined by allowing about 12cm (5in) for every cm (½in) of trunk diameter (see page 25). The fine roots should be left intact and the thickest roots severed. After the operation has been completed and the trench refilled, the plant may require the added support of a stake.

But finally, I must stress again that the pruning, whether restorative or more routine, of large trees in gardens isn't a matter for the gardener. It really is a task for a professional who will not only have experience to judge how much of which branches to remove, but also the knowledge to be sure where branches will fall; and, in the final analysis, will have the necessary insurance in case something does go amiss.

Sometimes you have to cut your losses; this *Weigela* is too feeble and congested to justify resurrection

PRUNING FOR ORNAMENTAL EFFECT

ABOVE: This *Wisteria sinensis* would not be remotely as eye-catching had it not been pruned correctly

RIGHT: The general vigour and flowering of this *Deutzia* x *magnifica* will be improved by the removal of some of the oldest shoots

The majority of garden plants, certainly the majority of shrubs, are grown for their ornamental value. We grow them because we like the look of them and we admire the way they complement other plants to create an overall attractive garden. This aesthetic value may be vested in flowers, foliage, bark, fruits or some other feature, and patently the plant will fail us if those features are produced

to less than their optimum. Pruning can sometimes be the means to ensure that the full value is obtained although, as I have mentioned elsewhere, it may not be the only answer. For instance, many shrubs may not flower well simply because they have been inadequately or inappropriately fed. Climbing plants are particularly amenable to having their flowering improved by pruning. Left to their own devices, they tend to produce upright shoots with flowers at the top and with large, dull and boring areas below. Apical dominance is to blame for this; the actively growing buds at the tips of the shoots suppress the development of those lower down. By a combination of bending vertical shoots to the horizontal and pruning off excess growth at the apex, however, flowers will be produced along the length of each shoot and will therefore cover the entire height of the wall or other support.

Sometimes, the ornamental appeal of a plant can be enhanced by not pruning; or at least by waiting before you do so. There are sound horticultural reasons for not pruning hydrangeas, for example, until the spring (see page 43) but there is an aesthetic benefit too, for the dead flowerheads can be extremely beautiful during the winter; far more beautiful than any neatly trimmed bush will ever be.

A shrub that has a mixture of new, slender shoots and thick, older ones, will be unlikely to be flowering to its optimum. Aesthetically a mass of stems is unattractive and a plant in this condition is certain to be functioning badly too, as almost no plants produce flower buds equally on young and old wood and none produce them in any quantity on very thick, very old woody stems. The regular removal of a proportion of the old stems will greatly increase the flower and fruit production and hence the appearance.

But flowering isn't the only way that a plant can render itself attractive. As *Best*

Foliage Shrubs demonstrates, leaves alone can be very appealing. And among foliage plants are the numerous varieties where the appeal comes from variegated leaves. Many of these commonly produce some shoots bearing green leaves only; this is sometimes called reversion. Pruning can help here too for the all-green shoots are invariably more vigorous and, left unchecked, will gradually supplant the variegated ones. Such reverted shoots should always be pruned out promptly.

Another, example of pruning for ornamental effect is seen in the many specimen trees or standard shrubs where the impact depends on a length of clear stem below the crown. The beautiful white barked Himalayan birches are perhaps the best of all instances of this and careful pruning away of embryo branches arising from the main stem

below the crown is essential. The sooner this is done, the better, as the more woody the young branch becomes, the greater will be the scar that it leaves.

Never forget the importance of an appealing shape. While appearance must never take precedence over horticulture (don't leave a diseased branch in place, even if it looks pretty), other things being equal, you should always prune to create a pleasing object. And do take your time over your pruning. Walk around the plant regularly during the operation to check that you are achieving a satisfying balance. Then the plant will look attractive and grow more productively.

By delaying the pruning of this *Hydrangea macrophylla* until the spring, the beauty of the plant is carried right through the winter

PRUNING FOR DAMAGE AND DISEASE CONTROL

In several places in the book, I've made reference to 'cutting out damaged or diseased branches'. Here, I want to look a little more closely at how far and how effectively the spread of problems can be limited by pruning. Again, I must stress that pruning can seldom be the entire answer and, as will be seen in *Best Garden Doctor*, many other considerations may need to be taken into account.

There are several important and distinct factors to consider. If a part of a plant has simply been damaged (a branch broken by a gale, bark scraped away by a lawnmower, a shrub trodden on), that damage won't spread. Complications may arise, however, if the broken tissues are invaded by a disease-causing fungus, as this may penetrate further into the plant and cause much more serious damage. Infection is less likely to take place if the initial wound is 'cleaned up' promptly and this is why I advise that branch stubs should be cut off cleanly, broken branches cut back to the basal collar (see page 25) and any damaged tissues cut back neatly to healthy wood or bark. Then the plant's natural healing processes will come into play and disease is much less likely to become established.

It's important, also, to recognise the difference between localised diseases and much more deep-seated or widespread problems. Most cankers are classic examples of localised problems: there isn't much infection beyond what can be seen. If the branch bearing the canker is cut away neatly, there should be no further spread along the same branch and you will also limit the number of spores being produced to initiate new infections elsewhere. (This doesn't guarantee that no more canker will occur because there may be spores in the air, blown from other trees nearby, but you will have made a significant difference.) By similar token, superficial diseases like some leaf spots and mildew may be limited if the

symptoms are spotted early in the season and the affected part snipped away. Later, control of mildew and especially of rusts is much harder because the diseases may become at least partly systemic; that is, the fungus will be present, hidden in the tissues, some way from the obvious symptoms.

Understanding a little of the biology of diseases will also help to indicate the value of pruning as a control. I've given

much more information on this in *Best Garden Doctor*, but one example will indicate the principle. Superficially, it might be thought that black spot on roses is best controlled by collecting up the diseased leaves. In practice, this will have little impact because once the leaves have dropped, the black spot fungus survives on them for a short while only. During the winter, it persists instead on small, more or less invisible lesions on the

blown to infect small dead twigs attached to living trees. On maples, for instance, normal winter wind and frost damage frequently causes the twig tips to die. Once established there, the coral spot fungus spreads downwards into the living tissues of the branch and can then cause serious dying-back. This example indicates the importance of two principles of pruning. First, don't leave old prunings in the garden; they could cause problems for you later. And second, look carefully at dead twigs and branches on trees and shrubs. If they are large, cut them off; if they are too small, numerous and twiggy to be removed wholesale, keep an eye open for any signs of coral spot or other fungal growth on them and remove immediately any that are affected.

BELOW: **The coral spot fungus grows on old pea sticks but can spread from there to attack living trees and shrubs**

ABOVE: **By pinching out the first mildewed apple shoots in the spring, the chances of the disease spreading are reduced**

LEFT: **By pruning out a canker, as on this old apple tree, you reduce the likelihood of the disease spreading to other trees**

shoots. Hard pruning in the spring to remove these diseased shoots is of much greater value.

There is one final consideration. A number of important diseases are caused by fungi that don't always attack living plants. The fungus that causes the familiar disease coral spot is a good example of this. It is equally capable of living on dead wood and is quite commonly seen on piles of old prunings and pea sticks left lying in the garden through the winter. Spores produced on these sticks are then

THE TIMING OF PRUNING

It is important to understand both the reasons for pruning and the best techniques to use. But all of this knowledge is useless if plants are pruned at the wrong time of the year. I feel that understanding the logic behind the timing of pruning transforms the mysterious in pruning into the methodical .

The single most important criterion to consider in deciding when to prune is flowering time. The second is the impact of the winter. And the third is the time of the year when the plant is growing most vigorously.

Let's look first at flowering time (and this is as important with plants grown for their fruit as those for their blossom alone). Flowering shrubs, trees and climbers bear their blooms in one of two ways. Either they bear them on wood produced during the previous growing season or they bear them on wood of the current year. But you don't need to know in depth the botany of all of your plants in order to discover this; commonsense will tell you. If a plant flowers early in the year, patently it cannot be on wood produced during that year; there will have been insufficient time for this to develop. So the flowers are borne on old wood: that produced in the previous or earlier years. Conversely, those plants that bloom later, after midsummer at least, bear their flowers on the current season's wood.

Clearly, you won't wish to remove the flower buds before they have had their chance to perform; so almost invariably, pruning is performed after flowering. But should you do so immediately after flowering, or wait a little longer? The general rule is that the early season, old wood flowerers are pruned immediately after the flowers fade. Rather few of this type require severe pruning. Many, like witch hazels and camellias require none and most of the remainder, like early flowering clematis, forsythia, winter-flowering jasmine and *Buddleja alternifolia*, need little more than a general tidying up of dead flowerheads.

By contrast, those that flower after midsummer on the wood of the current season should be pruned at some time between late autumn and late winter or early spring. Generally, the spring is preferable as the newly cut shoots are not then subjected to the rigours of winter and the possibility of frost penetrating through the pruning cuts. Leaving the old shoots on the plant over winter will also help provide protection

Wisterias should be pruned twice each year, the first time in late summer to shorten these long, whippy shoots

disease considerations restrict the time of pruning. The susceptibility of plums and related plants to silver-leaf disease is the classic example of this. The spores of the deadly silver-leaf fungus are produced in autumn and winter and infect through wounded tissues, including pruning cuts. It's for this reason that these plants should always be pruned in the spring or summer.

And finally, remember that timing considerations relate not just to leafy shoots but to other plant parts, too. The thinning-out of fruit or fruit bunches may need to be done at least once during the summer (page 90); and surplus flower buds may need to be removed at regular intervals on herbaceous plants like dahlias and chrysanthemums (page 93).

Grapes should be thinned out in order to produce the optimum crop

from the cold. By contrast with their spring-flowering counterparts, rather more of the late season flowerers need hard pruning. *Buddleja davidii* is a graphic example of this; it flowers late in the summer and requires cutting back almost to soil level in spring.

But there are sometimes other factors to consider. Plants like wisterias that are very vigorous may need pruning twice a year. If you try to make do with pruning once only, you will fall between two stools. Either you will prune too early and the plant will then put on a great deal more growth before the winter; or you will prune too late and the plant will, by then, have become an unruly tangle, and put of all of its energies into leaf, not flower, development. Hedges are special examples of this phenomenon, for we all want a hedge that develops fairly quickly and becomes dense and effective; but the price to pay for this is the need to clip several times. Remember, too, the old gardening adage that 'growth follows the knife'; in other words, the more you prune, the more you will have to prune, for each time, more and more dormant buds are stimulated into growth.

Vigour also determines the optimum pruning time in trees such as willows and walnuts. Here the sap flow in the plant in spring and early summer can be so strong that an astonishing amount is simply 'pumped out' through pruning cuts. Such sap loss can be seriously weakening as well as unsightly and should be taken account of when choosing the season to prune.

There are a few instances where

GENERAL PRUNING TECHNIQUES

Although there is a wide range of techniques available to a gardener embarking on the task of pruning, there are some that are relevant to almost everything he or she does; and they are not always easy to describe in words. Here, therefore, I have indicated diagrammatically the most important of them, together with the less familiar technique of notching/nicking that should be, I feel, better known and which is also best shown by illustration.

PRUNING CUTS

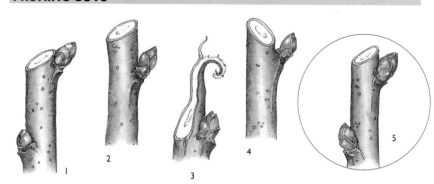

1. This is too close to the bud
2. This is too far from the bud
3. This is a careless cut with torn tissue
4. This cut is sloping the wrong way
5. A correct cut, not too close to the bud and sloping away from it.

HOW HARD SHOULD YOU PRUNE

The expressions that I probably use most in this book are 'hard pruning' and 'light pruning' and, unfortunately, they are also the most misunderstood. They aren't concerned with total matter cut away; they are concerned with proportions.

Light pruning Less than half of the stem is cut off. But remember that you may need to cut out some stems entirely and then only light prune the rest.

Hard pruning More than half (sometimes much more) of the stem is cut off; and quite commonly all the stems may need to be treated in this way.

DEAD-HEADING

Dead flowerheads are unsightly. They also attract diseases and may prevent new flowers from opening further down the stem. On annuals and other plants with many small blooms, snip them off wholesale. On shrubs like roses, with large, individual flowers, they should be removed more carefully.

Dead rhododendron flowers are unusual in that they should be pulled, not cut off to prevent damage to the new buds beneath.

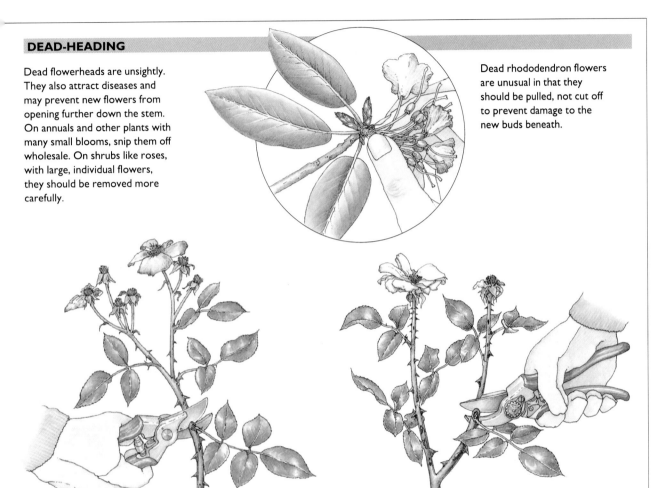

On Floribunda Roses, and similar shrubs with a flower cluster, cut back the entire flowering shoot. On roses, cut above a leaf with five, not three leaflets.

On Hybrid Tea Roses and similar shrubs, cut below the individual flowerhead to just above a plump, outward facing bud.

NOTCHING AND NICKING

Notching (left) entails making a small notch in the bark just above a dormant bud. This should encourage the bud to burst and avoid a length of bare stem. Nicking (right) consists of making a similar cut below a bud to prevent it from growing; this is useful when a plant is producing too many leafy shoots.

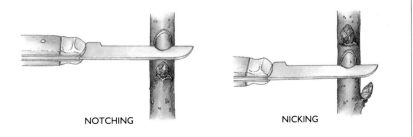

NOTCHING

NICKING

PRUNING AND FLOWERING TIME

*I*n many of the individual plant entries in the book, I refer to the timing of pruning in relation to the time of flowering. On page 16, I explain the importance of this in terms of the type of wood on which the flowers are borne: on the wood produced in the current season or on the wood produced last year or the year before. On these pages,

I have illustrated some of the most important instructions that occur elsewhere in the book. These also illustrate the value of having more than the very basic tools for your pruning operations. When the instruction is to 'trim' rather than to 'prune', the implication is that shears are the most appropriate tool. Double or single-handed shears are both useful but single-handed

sheers permit you to hold a tuft of shoots whilst cutting. Pruning either before flowering or a long time afterwards could mean that you have to cut through fairly tough wood and you may find anvil pattern secateurs more appropriate. When pruning immediately after flowering, the chances are that the tissues will be fairly soft, and scissor action secateurs will be suitable.

TRIM AFTER FLOWERING

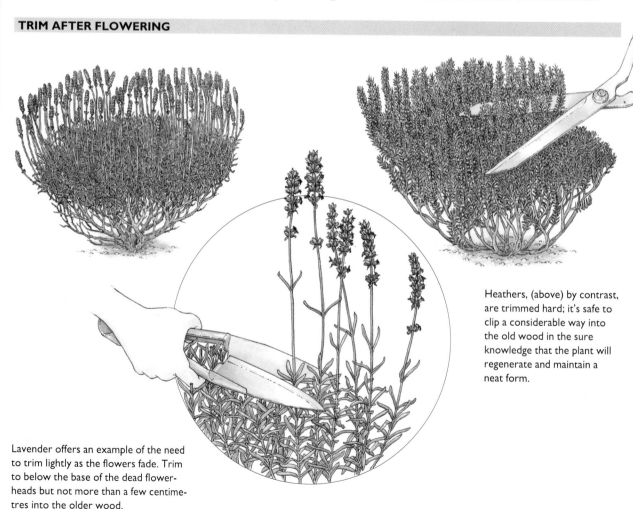

Heathers, (above) by contrast, are trimmed hard; it's safe to clip a considerable way into the old wood in the sure knowledge that the plant will regenerate and maintain a neat form.

Lavender offers an example of the need to trim lightly as the flowers fade. Trim to below the base of the dead flower-heads but not more than a few centimetres into the older wood.

PRUNE BEFORE FLOWERING

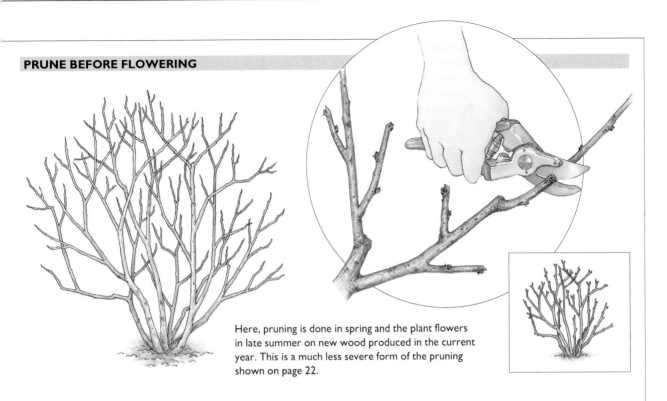

Here, pruning is done in spring and the plant flowers in late summer on new wood produced in the current year. This is a much less severe form of the pruning shown on page 22.

REMOVE DEAD FLOWERED SHOOTS

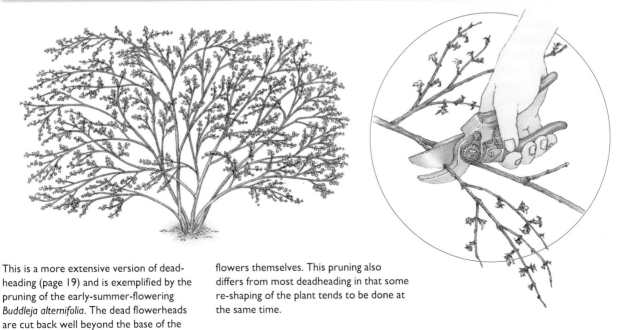

This is a more extensive version of dead-heading (page 19) and is exemplified by the pruning of the early-summer-flowering *Buddleja alternifolia*. The dead flowerheads are cut back well beyond the base of the flowers themselves. This pruning also differs from most deadheading in that some re-shaping of the plant tends to be done at the same time.

PRUNING AND FLOWERING TIME/STOOLING

*P*lants that flower after mid-summer generally require pruning rather more severely. This may entail cutting back the entire plant to just above soil level in early spring. It looks just too drastic to be doing any good, but Leycesteria, Rhus typhina *and* Buddleja davidii *as well as autumn-fruiting raspberries are among those that require it.*

The technique is also used for those plants like some Cornus *varieties and willows where the* appeal or usefulness of the plant lies in the production of a mass of young stems. It then tends to be called stooling. It may be compared with the similar operation of cutting back to a main trunk, known as pollarding (page 24).

STOOLING OR CUTTING BACK TO SOIL LEVEL

It's important not to cut back the flowering shrubs too early in the spring or they may suffer frost damage to the crown. Although the precise time will vary depending on where you live, try to choose a period when the worst of the winter frosts are past but new shoot growth has not yet begun.

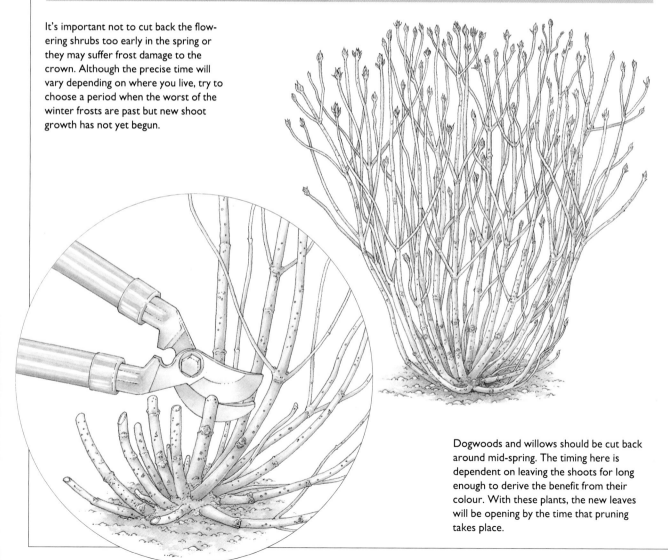

Dogwoods and willows should be cut back around mid-spring. The timing here is dependent on leaving the shoots for long enough to derive the benefit from their colour. With these plants, the new leaves will be opening by the time that pruning takes place.

RENEWAL PRUNING BY REMOVING A PROPORTION OF THE STEMS ANNUALLY

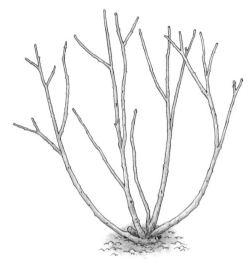

1. This shrub has been neglected but with annual renewal pruning, it can be rejuvenated. You need to remember the 'rule of three': the oldest one-third of the stems are cut out each year in spring.

2. The first year's work is complete; the oldest one-third of the stems have gone. The other stems have been pruned only very lightly as the intention is to stimulate new growth from the base.

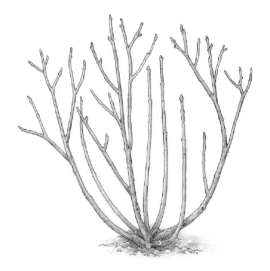

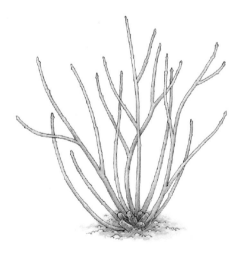

3. One year on, new shoots have emerged from the base. These won't be pruned but the oldest one-third of the shoots can now be cut out; as four old ones remain, one of them should now be taken out.

4. After a further year, more new shoots have been produced and the remaining three old ones can now be cut out. Hereafter, the removal of the oldest one-third of the shoots each spring means that the plant will be entirely renewed every three years.

TECHNIQUES WITH TREES

*S*ome of the techniques illustrated on the preceding pages play a part in the overall shaping of garden plants. Shaping can be a more deliberate operation, however, and it is especially necessary with trees. And most important of all with fruit trees. Here are three important shapes for a free-standing tree. The original planting stock was the same for each but, because of selective removal of particular shoots, the final form of the trees differs widely. The bush is produced by cutting short the leader, allowing the proliferation of laterals from around the point of the cut and removing those arising lower down. The pyramid is produced by less drastic shortening of the leader and by leaving the laterals over a much greater proportion of the overall length. The standard is produced by almost no shortening of the leader and by selective removal of laterals. To illustrate the difference in maintenance, the lines show the parts to be pruned off apple trees of each type during the winter.

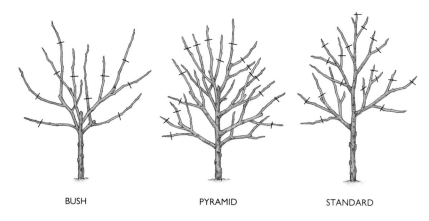

BUSH   PYRAMID   STANDARD

POLLARDING

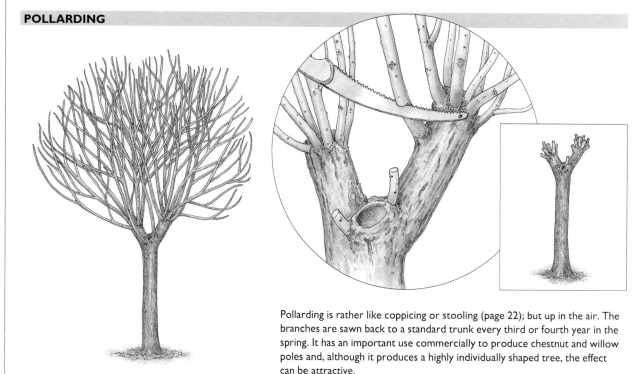

Pollarding is rather like coppicing or stooling (page 22); but up in the air. The branches are sawn back to a standard trunk every third or fourth year in the spring. It has an important use commercially to produce chestnut and willow poles and, although it produces a highly individually shaped tree, the effect can be attractive.

ROOT PRUNING

Root pruning is most commonly used to diminish the vigour of apple, pear or some ornamental trees but should never be done on plums or other *Prunus* species, willows or poplars as they will respond by excessive production of suckers. Root pruning is achieved by carefully digging a circular trench in autumn approximately 45cm (18in) deep and at a radius from the trunk determined by allowing about 12cm (5in) for every 1cm (½in) of trunk diameter. The fine roots should be left intact and the thickest roots severed.

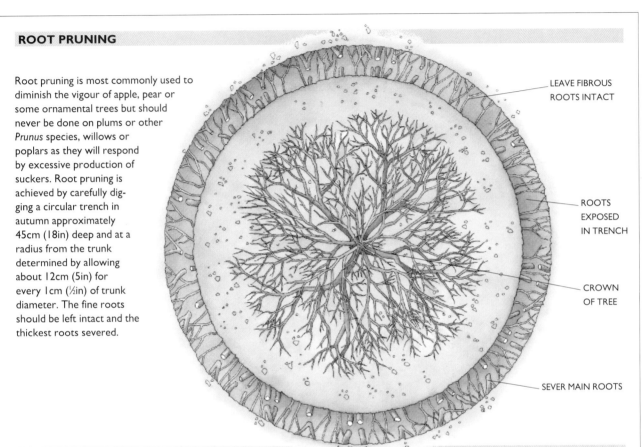

LEAVE FIBROUS ROOTS INTACT

ROOTS EXPOSED IN TRENCH

CROWN OF TREE

SEVER MAIN ROOTS

BRANCH REMOVAL

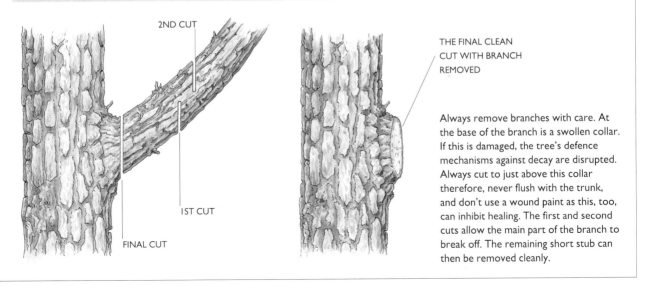

2ND CUT

1ST CUT

FINAL CUT

THE FINAL CLEAN CUT WITH BRANCH REMOVED

Always remove branches with care. At the base of the branch is a swollen collar. If this is damaged, the tree's defence mechanisms against decay are disrupted. Always cut to just above this collar therefore, never flush with the trunk, and don't use a wound paint as this, too, can inhibit healing. The first and second cuts allow the main part of the branch to break off. The remaining short stub can then be removed cleanly.

CLIMBERS

I always feel that the big problem gardeners have in pruning climbers is due to a basic misunderstanding of the way they grow. If only people would think of climbers as long spindly shrubs that happen to need some support, they would be less wary of tackling them. All of the basic pruning principles that I've out-

lined already are equally applicable to climbing plants. The relationship between pruning and flowering, and the relationship between severity of pruning and the time of year of flowering are just the same. The plant that I've chosen to illustrate this is the archetypal climber; the most popular of all and yet also the one at which most people balk, the

clematis. The fact that clematis can be divided into three main groups for pruning purposes tends to add to the confusion although, in reality, this sub-division helps to demonstrate the basic principles of pruning. As you will see, there is a rule of thumb: the later in the year that the clematis flowers, the harder it should be pruned.

GROUP I

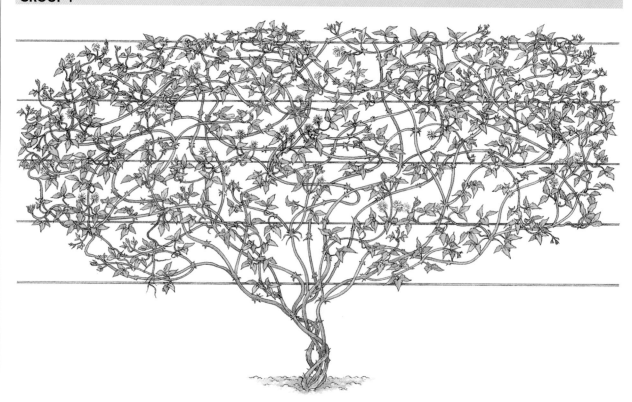

Group I types flower early in the year but on wood produced in the previous season. Prune immediately after flowering by cutting back all weak and dead stems to just above a node. Any tangled or excessive growth should also be cut back, but large, well established plants that are growing where they may be allowed free rein need not be pruned at all. Conversely, a plant that has truly become a tangled mass may be pruned back as hard as a Group 2 or even a Group 3 plant and will regenerate successfully although, in the latter case, all of one year's flower buds will, of course, be removed.

GROUP 2

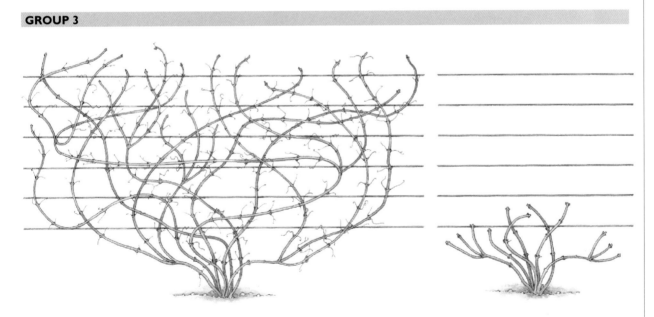

Group 2 types flower early in the summer and, like the Group 1 varieties, they also flower on the previous season's wood and, like them, should be pruned in early spring by cutting out any dead or weak stems. As they flower rather later, however, they require rather harder pruning, so cut back the remaining shoots by about 30cm (12in), cutting to just above a pair of plump buds. Any dead leaf stalks should be trimmed away and the plant generally tidied up

GROUP 3

Group 3 types flower later in the summer on the current year's wood and they should also be pruned early in the spring but, flowering later, should be pruned much more severely. All of the previous season's growth should be cut back to just above a pair of plump buds positioned about 75cm (30in) above soil level. If there is so much top growth that it will be blown around in the winter, however, the bulk may be cut back in late autumn, leaving the final tidying until the early spring.

SPECIALISED FRUIT PRUNING

*There are three methods of train-
ing that are especially, although
not exclusively, valuable with tree
fruit. All three, cordons, espaliers
and fans, entail removing some laterals and tying others in such a way
that the whole plant takes on a more
or less two-dimensional form. This
confers three advantages: the whole
occupies less space, the fruit are easier to pick and, if the plants are
trained against a wall, all the shoots
are sheltered by it. The illustrations
here show trees of each type as they
should appear, almost fully established, in the late summer. I hope
that reference to these ideals will
enable the pruning and training
advice that appears later in the
book to be followed more usefully.*

Cordon (apple) The laterals on the upper
side of the main stem tend to be more vigorous than those beneath. All laterals longer
than 20cm (8in) should now be cut back to a
point just above the third leaf cluster from
the base. If this is done too early, further
unwanted growth will be produced before
the autumn.

Espalier (pear) As with the cordon, any laterals
more than 20cm (8in) long are ready to be cut back
while the sub-laterals will be cut back to one leaf.
Almost all last year's extension growth on the lower
arms was cut back in late spring. That on the upper
arms were left as the shoots have yet to fill their
allotted space.

Fan (peach) The laterals were thinned out in spring to about 10cm (4in) apart. Most sub-laterals have been pinched back to six or seven leaves although some have been left to fill in the remaining gaps in the fan. Those shoots over-topping the wall will be shortened to six leaves; by autumn, they should again just reach the top.

29

TREES, SHRUBS AND CLIMBERS

Abies Silver fir

Size if unpruned: The most popular garden species, *Abies koreana*, often sold as a dwarf, will eventually attain about 10 x 5m (33 x 16ft) but it does grow very slowly. Among other common silver firs, the true dwarf, *A. balsamea* f. *hudsonia* will reach only 60cm-1m x 60cm-1m (24in-3ft x 24in x 3ft); *A. concolor* 'Compacta' will reach about 4-5 x 1.5-2m (13-16 x 5-6½ft); *A. veitchii* about 15 x 5m (50 x 16ft) while *A. grandis* is a big tree and will reach about 30 x 11m (100 x 36ft).
Pruning: Any lateral shoot competing with the central leader on young trees should be cut back to the basal collar as early as possible (page 25). Apart from that, pruning is to be discouraged.

Abutilon

Size if unpruned: The most popular and overall hardiest species, *Abutilon vitifolium* will attain 4 x 2m (13 x 6½ft) after five years, and 6 x 4m (20 x 13ft) after 20 years.
Pruning: None necessary although there will almost always be some winter-damaged shoots which should be cut back to healthy wood in the spring.

Acer Maple

Size if unpruned: Among common and popular larger maples, *Acer cappadocicum*, *A. platanoides* and *A. rubrum* will reach about 6 x 3m (20 x 10ft) after five years and 20 x 12-15m (65 x 40-50ft) after 20 years; *A. griseum*, *A. negundo*, *A. saccharinum* and the snake-bark maples will reach only a third to a half of this size, and *A. pseudoplatanus* 'Brilliantissimum' about 2.5 x 1.5m (8 x 5ft) after five years and 4.5 x 3.5m (15 x 11ft) after 20 years. The beautiful Oriental maples tend to be rather smaller: the *A. japonicum* varieties and *A. shirasawanum* 'Aureum' will reach

about 1 x 1.8m (3 x 6ft) after five years and 2.5 x 3m (8 x 10ft) after 20 years. *A. palmatum* will reach about 2 x 2m (6½ x 6½ft) after five years and 5 x 5m (16 x 16ft) after 20 years, but most of its named varieties slightly less than this and the 'Dissectum' group is very slow-growing and will eventually reach only 1.5 x 2 m (5 x 6½ft).
Pruning: None essential and generally to be discouraged because of the likelihood of infection by coral spot disease. However, young branches (up to about three years old) may be cut back if desired to reduce the size of the tree and on varieties with interesting bark, lower branches may be removed to enhance the appearance. This should be done in late summer or early autumn.

Actinidia

Size if unpruned: *Actinidia kolomikta* will reach about 1.5 x 1.5m (5 x 5ft) after five years and 6 x 6m (20 x 20ft) eventually.
Pruning: Cut out any untidy stems in summer. In winter all side-shoots should be pruned back to about 5cm (2in) from

their junction with the main stems. For *A. chinensis*, the Kiwi fruit, see page 91.

Akebia Chocolate vine

Size if unpruned: The most common species, *Akebia quinata*, will reach 1.8 x 1.8m (6 x 6ft) after five years, and 6 x 9m (20 x 30ft) after 20 years.
Pruning: Little is needed, but every few years overgrown plants may be cut back hard in spring (page 27).

Amelanchier Snowy mespil, June berry

Size if unpruned: *Amelanchier lamarckii* will reach 4.5 x 3m (15 x 10ft) after five years, and 7.5 x 6m (24 x 20ft) after 20 years.
Pruning: None essential, but the lower shoots may be removed if desired. *A. canadensis*, which is inferior as a garden tree, will sucker profusely and these must be pulled out regularly.

Ampelopsis

Size if unpruned: *Ampelopsis glandulosa* var. *brevipedunculata* will reach about 1.5 x 1.5m (5 x 5ft) after five years and then 6 x 6m (20 x 20ft) after 20 years, and its form 'Elegans' about three-quarters of this size.
Pruning: *A. glandulosa* var. *brevipedunculata* requires only tidying, but will withstand being cut back hard in late winter or early spring if this is necessary to limit spread. 'Elegans' should have all the previous season's side shoots cut back to within two buds of their base to encourage the growth of new pink foliage.

***Actinidia kolomikta* foliage with good leaf colouration, encouraged with careful pruning**

ABOVE: *Amelanchier canadensis* is much more prone than *A. lamarckii* to produce suckers

Araucaria Monkey puzzle tree

Size if unpruned: *Araucaria araucana* will attain about 1.2m x 80cm (4ft x 32in) after 10 years, and 20 x 15m (65 x 50ft) eventually.
Pruning: None essential although lower branches tend to die back on older trees and should be cut back to the trunk in spring.

Arbutus Strawberry tree

Size if unpruned: 1 x 1m (3 x 3ft) after five years, and 5 x 5m (16 x 16ft) after 20 years.
Pruning: None necessary

Arctostaphylos

Size if unpruned: The popular ground-cover varieties, such as *Arctostaphylos uva-ursi* and *A. nevadensis* which are about 50cm (20in) high, will eventually spread to about 1m (3ft).
Pruning: None necessary.

Aristolochia Dutchman's pipe

Size if unpruned: *Aristolochia durior* will reach 1.8 x 1.2m (6 x 4ft) after five years; 6 x 6m (20 x 20ft) after 20 years.
Pruning: None essential, but untidy shoots may be cut back in early summer after flowering.

BELOW: **The appearance of a mature *Araucaria araucana* is often spoiled by the presence of dead lower branches**

Artemisia

Size if unpruned: *Artemisia abrotanum* will reach its full height of about 80cm (32in) and a spread of 80cm (32in) after five years, and will spread to about 1.2m (4ft) after 20 years.
Pruning: The shrubby species, such as *A. abrotanum*, or Southernwood, need only tidying by removal of winter damaged shoots in early spring. They are almost always browned unattractively. See also herbaceous plants page 92.

Atriplex
Tree purslane

Size if unpruned: *Atriplex halimus* will reach its full height of about 1.2m (4ft) and a spread of about 1.2m (4ft) after five years and will spread to about 1.8m (6ft) eventually.
Pruning: None essential but cut back hard any frost-damaged shoots into healthy wood in early spring (page 18).

Aucuba
Spotted laurel

Size if unpruned: 1.2 x 1.2m (4 x 4ft) after five years, and about 4 x 4m (13 x 13ft) after 20 years.
Pruning: None essential but may suffer in severe drought and damaged branches should then be cut back hard in the following spring (page 18). Blackening of shoot tips is quite common and these should be cut back by half during spring or summer.

Berberis darwinii will flower satisfactorily for several years without pruning

Berberis Barberry

Size if unpruned: Medium forms such as *Berberis julianae* and *B.* x *stenophylla* will reach 1.5 x 1.5m (5 x 5ft) after five years and 4 x 4m (13 x 13ft) eventually; *B. thunbergii* about 1.8 x 1.5m (6 x 5ft) after five years and 2.7 x 3m (9 x 10ft) after 20 years; taller forms such as *B. darwinii* and *B. lologensis* will reach about 2.7 x 2.7m (9 x 9ft) eventually.
Pruning: None essential but old plants will benefit from having the oldest one-third of the shoots cut out in spring (p. 23). The occasional tall and wayward shoots on small plants should be cut back to the base at the same time (p. 18). For hedges, see p. 65.

Betula Birch

Size if unpruned: The popular weeping *Betula pendula* 'Youngii' will reach about 4 x 1m (13 x 3ft) after five years and 8 x 10m (25 x 30ft) after 20 years; the other common white-barked forms will reach about 6 x 1.5m (20 x 5ft) after five years and 12 x 5m (40 x 16ft) after 20 years. Many quite naturally develop two or three distinct trunks.
Pruning: None essential, but lower branches may be removed, ideally in autumn, to enhance the appearance of the trunk (page 13). In general, however, pruning of birches should be kept to a minimum because of the high risk of infection by decay fungi.

Bignonia Trumpet vine, Cross vine

Size if unpruned: 2m (6½ft) after three years; up to 15m (50ft) eventually.
Pruning: In spring remove any frost-damaged shoots (page 18) and, if necessary to limit size, cut back all of the previous season's growth by between half and two-thirds (page 22).

Buddleja (including Butterfly bush)

Size if unpruned: *Buddleja alternifolia* will reach 6 x 6m (20 x 20ft), the other common species including *B. davidii* 3-4 x 3-4m (10-13 x 10-13ft).
Pruning: Differs for different species. *B. alternifolia*, if grown informally, should have its flowering shoots cut back to the base immediately after the flowers have faded, and the oldest shoots removed at the same time (page 21). If grown as a standard, remove the flowering shoots in the same way and maintain the weeping habit by removing any stray shoots in autumn and again after flowering (page 21). *B. globosa* should be lightly pruned after flowering (page 21). The other species, which flower on the current year's growth, should have all stems cut back to about 15cm (6in) above soil level at end of winter (page 22); or they may be grown on a permanent framework of stems up to 1m (3ft) high, in which case

Buddleja davidii does look rather 'butchered' after its spring pruning

they are cut back at the same time to about 15cm (6in) above this old wood.

Buxus Box

Size if unpruned: *Buxus sempervirens* will reach 1 x 1m (3 x 3ft) after five years and 4 x 4m (13 x 13ft) after 20 years. *B. microphylla* will eventually reach about 1 x 1.5m (3 x 5ft); and the dwarf variety, *B. sempervirens* 'Suffruticosa', will reach only 75 x 75cm (30 x 30in).
Pruning: None essential if grown informally, but old plants may be rejuvenated by being cut hard back in mid-spring (page 18). For hedges and topiary see pages 63 and 66.

Callistemon Bottlebrush

Size if unpruned: 2 x 1.5m (6½ x 5ft) after five years and twice this after 20 years.
Pruning: None essential, but mature, very woody or misshapen plants may be rejuvenated by cutting hard back in spring.

Calluna Heather

Size if unpruned: Most varieties are low growing, between 10 and 50cm (4 and 20in), and hummock-forming, spreading to about 50cm (20in).
Pruning: Remove dead flowerheads with shears, cutting fairly hard to just above the old wood (page 21). For those varieties grown primarily for their winter foliage this should be done in mid- to late autumn. Others may be left until spring as the dead flower heads can be attractive in the winter. All heathers are prone to become very woody and straggly after five or more years and pruning is not then the answer; obtain new plants.

Campsis **need only be pruned when trained against a wall**

Camellia

Size if unpruned: Most are slow-growing and will reach their ultimate size of about 3-4 x 2-3m (10-13 x 6½-10ft) in 15 to 20 years.
Pruning: None essential, but any misplaced or untidy branches may be cut out after flowering, cutting back to the parent shoot (page 21). Dead flowerheads should be pulled off.

Campsis Trumpet vine

Size if unpruned: *Campsis radicans* will reach 3 x 3m (10 x 10ft) after five years, and 9 x 9m (30 x 30ft) after 20 years; *C. grandiflora,* in favourable conditions, will reach slightly less than this size after five years and slightly more after 20 years.

Pruning: None essential if grown informally, but when trained against a wall the plants should be allowed to establish a permanent framework of stems and then have all side-shoots pruned to within 5cm (2in) of this in spring.

Caragana Pea tree

Size if unpruned: The common varieties of *Caragana arborescens* are usually top-grafted on to stems of 1, 1.5 or 2m (3, 5 or 6½ft), and will make trees of 2-3 x 1-2m (6½-10 x 3-6½ft) eventually.
Pruning: None essential, but young trees may be pruned hard every three or four years in spring to encourage new growth (page 18). The plants benefit from being well staked as they have pliable stems and easily develop distorted.

Carpenteria

Size if unpruned: The only species, *Carpenteria californica* will reach its ultimate height of about 2 x 1.5m (6½ x 5ft) after about five years.

Pruning: After flowering (or in early summer if flowering continues, as it may), cut back the old flowered shoots (page 21) and cut out any misplaced shoots. At the same time, remove up to one-quarter of the oldest shoots, cutting back to a few centimetres above soil level (page 23).

Caryopteris

Size if unpruned: About 60 x 80cm (24 x 32in) after five years; 80 x 80cm (32 x 32in) eventually.

Pruning: Cut back all shoots almost to soil level in mid- to late spring each year (page 22).

Catalpa Indian bean tree

Size if unpruned: *Catalpa bignonioides* will reach 5 x 5m (16 x 15ft) after five years; 12 x 12m (40 x 40ft) after 20 years.
Pruning: None essential and only branches damaged or broken should be removed (page 25)

Ceanothus

Size if unpruned: Most deciduous forms will reach about 1.5 x 1.5m (5 x 5ft) after five years and 2.5 x 2.5m (8 x8ft) after 20 years. Evergreen types often grow larger, reaching 2 x 2m (6½ x 6½ft) after five years and 4 x 4m (13 x 13ft) after 20 years.
Pruning: Evergreen varieties grown as free-standing shrubs should have dead shoots cut out in spring and any wayward or misplaced shoots tidied up after flowering. When early-flowering evergreen types are grown as wall shrubs, they should be pruned harder after

flowering; to within three buds of the previous season's growth. Deciduous varieties should be pruned hard in spring, also to within three buds of the previous season's growth.

Cedrus Cedar

Size if unpruned: The species will reach a height of 25m (82ft) eventually, and a spread of 10-15m (33 x 50ft); among the smallest of the common cultivated forms is *Cedrus deodara* 'Aurea' which will reach only 5 x 4m (16 x 13ft) eventually.
Pruning: Any lateral shoots competing with the central leader on young trees should be removed as they arise and until the required height is reached. The wood is brittle and the leader is prone to be blown out in winter gales; if this occurs, a lateral shoot should be selected and left to form a new leader (page 6).

Celastrus Bittersweet

Size if unpruned: *Celastrus orbiculatus* will reach 3 x 3m (10 x 10ft) after five years and 9 x 9m (30 x 30ft) after 20 years; *C. scandens* reaches slightly more than this.

Although evergreen *Ceanothus* 'Cynthia Postan' (LEFT) and deciduous *C.* 'Perle Rose' (RIGHT) are similar in flowering appearance, the pruning needed to achieve these ends is rather different

Pruning: None essential, but these are vigorous plants and easily outgrow their owner's expectations. Fortunately, mature plants withstand being cut back hard in early spring (page 18). They may be cut back to as little as 1m (3ft) above soil level without fear of harm.

Ceratostigma Shrubby plumbago

Size if unpruned: *Ceratostigma willmottianum* will reach about 60 x 60cm (24 x 24in) after five years and 1 x 1m (3 x 3ft) after 20 years; *C. griffithii* somewhat less than this.
Pruning: To prevent the plants from becoming woody and untidy, cut back all shoots to just above soil level in mid-spring (page 22); don't prune in autumn as the dead growth provides valuable protection against winter cold.

Cercis Judas tree

Size if unpruned: 1.5 x 1.5m (5 x 5ft) after five years, and 6 x 6m (20 x 20ft) after 20 years.

Pruning: None essential, but well established plants may have unwanted or misplaced branches removed (page 25).

Chaenomeles Japanese quince

Size if unpruned: Most varieties will reach up to 2 x 2m (6½ x 6½ft) after five years and their full size of 3 x 3m (10 x 10ft) after 10 years.

Pruning: On free-standing plants, thin out overcrowded shoots in the centre (page 7) and cut back the previous season's growth by about one-third after flowering (page 18). On wall-trained plants, cut back the previous season's growth to two or three buds from the base after flowering, and remove any shoots growing directly towards or away from the wall. In a very confined space, the side-shoots may be cut back to 3-4cm (1¼ - 1½in) from their bases to form spurs (page 7).

Chamaecyparis Falsecypress

Size if unpruned: There is a considerable range; among common varieties, *Chamaecyparis lawsoniana* 'Ellwoodii' will reach about 3m x 80cm (10ft x 32in); 'Ellwood's Gold', 2m x 45cm (6 1/2ft x 18in); 'Minima Aurea' and 'Minima Glauca' about 1 x 1m (3 x 3ft); *C. pisifera* 'Boulevard' will reach about 5 x 3m (16 x 10ft) eventually.

Pruning: Any lateral shoots competing with the central leader on young trees should be removed as they arise and until the required height is reached (page 6). Narrowly upright forms are best wired to prevent them from opening outwards,

especially after strong winds or snowfalls. For hedges see page 64.

Clematis

Size if unpruned: The most vigorous forms, such as *Clematis montana,* will reach 4.5 x 4.5m (15 x 15ft) after five years and 9 x 9m (30 x 30ft) after 20 years; *C. tangutica* will reach about half this size; and *C. alpina* will reach its maximum size of about 2.5 x 2.5m (8 x 8ft) after five years.

Pruning: Clematis are divided into three groups for pruning: Group 1 includes evergreens and varieties derived from *C. alpina, C. macropetala* and *C. montana,* all of which flower early in the year, on the previous year's wood. They should, where possible, be tidied after flowering, by removing all weak and dead stems to just above a pair of strong buds (page 26). But where space allows, large, mature specimens need not be pruned at all. Group 2 includes the summer-flowering hybrids of *C. florida, C. patens* and *C. lanuginosa,* which also flower on the previous year's growth. They need to be pruned in early spring, before they flower,

to keep them tidy and to encourage new growth. Any dead or weak stems should be removed completely (page 27). Remaining stems should be cut back by about 25-30cm (10-12in), to a strong pair of buds. Group 3 includes the late-flowering hybrids of *C.* 'Jackmanii' and *C. viticella,* and late-flowering species such as *C. tangutica.* They flower on the current season's wood, and their top growth dies back during the winter. They require the most drastic pruning: in early spring the plant should be cut back to just above a pair of strong buds about 75cm (30in) above soil level (page 27).

I should add, nonetheless, that all clematis can be pruned hard if they have been neglected and become overgrown. One season's flowers may be lost but the plant will be rejuvenated. Only if a very old plant has developed a massive trunk

Early flowering *Clematis montana* (LEFT) is best left unpruned and informal; the large summer flowering hybrid (RIGHT) requires much more careful attention

Choisya Mexican orange blossom

Size if unpruned: *Choisya ternata* will reach 1 x 1.2m (3 x 4ft) after five years and 2 x 2m (6½ x 6½ft) after 20 years; the yellowish-leaved 'Sundance' will grow to about two-thirds of this size.
Pruning: Remove any frost-damaged shoots in mid-spring, then cut out the oldest one-third of the shoots from the base immediately after flowering (page 23).

Cornus (including Dogwood)

Size if unpruned: Among common flowering types, *Cornus florida, C. mas* and *C. kousa* will reach about 2 x 2m (6½ x 6½ft) after five years and after 20 years may grow to 8-10 x 8-10m (25-30 x 25-30ft). Most of the upright foliage varieties will reach about 2 x 3m (6½ x 10ft) after five years and about 3 x 4m (10 x 13ft) after 20 years; *C. canadensis,* which is

Hard spring pruning is essential to encourage the coloured young shoots on *Cornus stolonifera* 'Flaviramea'

about 20cm (8in) high, will spread to about 3m (10ft) eventually.
Pruning: None essential with those types grown for flower, but *C. mas* may be lightly pruned to keep it to a required size (page 18). To produce their colourful new winter shoots, all the stems of *C. alba* and *C. stolonifera* should be cut back to about 20cm (8in) above soil level in mid-spring each year (page 22). *C. florida* and *C. canadensis* require no pruning.

The new shoots of purple hazel *Corylus maxima* 'Purpurea' have the best foliage colour and are encouraged by selective pruning

Corylus Hazel

Size if unpruned: Of the two commonest ornamental hazels, *Corylus avellana* 'Contorta' is slow-growing and will eventually reach 3 x 4m (10 x 13ft); *C. maxima* 'Purpurea' is more vigorous and will reach about 3 x 3m (10 x 10ft) after five years and 6 x 6m (20 x 20ft) after 20 years.
Pruning: *C. avellana* 'Contorta' is most attractive when left unpruned although any misplaced shoots may be cut out after flowering in spring (page 21). *C. maxima* 'Purpurea' should be pruned hard in late winter or early spring to encourage more prolific foliage. Much the best way is to cut out the oldest one-third of the shoots (page 23)

Cotinus Smoke bush

Size if unpruned: 1.5 x 1.8m (5 x 6ft) after five years; 6 x 6m (20 x 20ft) after 20 years.
Pruning: None essential, but it is wise occasionally to cut out the oldest branches in spring to promote new growth (page 23). The plants will tolerate being cut entirely down to soil level in spring (page 22), but while it will produce more vigorous foliage, the number of flowers will be diminished.

Cotoneaster

Size if unpruned: There is a considerable range. Among the varieties grown mainly for flowers and fruit, *Cotoneaster conspicuus* will grow only to about 1.2 x 2.5m (4 x 8ft) at maturity; *C.* 'Cornubia' will reach 6 x 6m (20 x 20ft); while forms of *C. salicifolius* such as 'Rothschildianus' may even reach 7 x 7m (23 x 23ft). The ground-cover foliage plants, such as the evergreen *C. microphyllus,* will reach a maximum height of about 50cm (20in) and spread to about 2m (6½ft) after five years, and 3m (10ft) after 20 years; *C. horizontalis* will reach about 1 x 3m (3 x 10ft) eventually.
Pruning: None essential if grown informally but most cotoneasters can very attractively be trained as standards (page 24). The smaller-leaved foliage types may be used as hedges (see page 65).

Crataegus Thorn, Hawthorn

Size if unpruned: *Crataegus monogyna,* the common hawthorn will reach 10 x 8m (30 x 25ft).
Pruning: None essential if grown informally; for hedges see page 63. When allowed to form standard trees, it will be necessary to remove young branches to maintain a clear length of trunk.

Crinodendron Lantern tree

Size if unpruned: *Crinodendron hookerianum*, the most familiar species, will reach 10 x 3m (30 x 10ft) in favourably mild areas.

Pruning: None essential although branches browned by winter cold should be cut back into healthy wood in the spring (page 25).

Cupressus/ x Cupressocyparis Cypress

Size if unpruned: Among popular *Cupressus* species, *C. arizonica* will reach about 10-15 x 3-5m (33-50 x 10-16ft) eventually, and its varieties will vary from this size. *C. macrocarpa* will reach about 20 x 6-25m (65 x 20-80ft), as it is columnar when young, but tends to spread when mature; varieties vary widely. The Leyland Cypress, x *Cupressocyparis leylandi,* will reach about 30 x 7m (100 x 23ft); the more or less golden-foliaged varieties about two-thirds to three-quarters of this size.

Pruning: None essential, but the lowest branches may be removed so as to give a clear trunk that will enhance the appearance of specimen trees (page 13). Any lateral shoots competing with the central leader on young trees should be removed as soon as possible (page 6). See also hedges page 64.

Cytisus Broom

Size if unpruned: *Cytisus battandieri* will reach about 3 x 2m (10 x 6½ft) after five years, and about 6 x 6m (20 x 20ft) after 20 years; *C. x kewensis* will reach about 50 x 80cm (20 x 32in) after five years and spread to about 1.5m (5ft) after 20 years; *C. x praecox* 'Allgold' will reach about 80cm x 1m (32in x 3ft) after five years

A small 'tree' can be created by training a multi-stemmed shrub like *Cotoneaster salicifolius* 'Rothschildianus' as a standard

and 1.2 x 2m (4 x 6½ft) after 20 years.

Pruning: None essential, but cutting back old flowered shoots after flowering will encourage new growth (page 21). *C. battandieri* can be trained against a wall by removing shoots growing directly towards and away from the support. I have seen it trained most attractively as an espalier (page 78).

Daphne

Size if unpruned: Most daphnes are low to medium in height. *Daphne odora* will reach about 50 x 80cm (20 x 32in) after five years and 1.8 x 1m (6 x 3ft) after 20 years. *Daphne tangutica* will reach about 10 x 30cm (4 x 12in) after five years and 80 x 80cm (32 x 32in) after 20 years.

Pruning: None essential and the removal of misplaced or damaged shoots should

be done by cutting back in spring to the parent shoot (page 25) or die-back may easily ensue.

Danae Alexandrian laurel

Size if unpruned: 60 x 80cm (24 x 32in) after five years; 1 x 1.8m (3 x 6ft) after 20 years.

Pruning: None essential but may be trimmed with shears in spring (page 20).

Decumaria

Size if unpruned: 1.5 x 1.5m (5 x 5ft) after five years; 6 x 6m (20 x 20ft) after 20 years.

Pruning: None essential but if growing in a confined space, excess growth may be cut back in spring.

Desfontainea

Size if unpruned: The only species, *Desfontainea spinosa* will reach 2m (6½ft) after five years and 3m (10ft) eventually.
Pruning: None normally needed; may be lightly trimmed in late spring to retain or restore shape (page 18).

Diervilla
Bush honeysuckle

Size if unpruned: 1.5 x 1.5m (5 x 5ft) after five years and 3.5 x 3.5m (11 x 11ft) after 20 years.
Pruning: *D. sessilifolia* may be treated as an herbaceous plant, and cut back to ground level each spring (paage 92). Mature plants of this and other species grown as shrubs may be rejuvenated by removing two- and three-year-old stems at ground level after flowering (page 23).

All-green shoots on variegated plants such as *Elaeagnus pungens* 'Maculata' must be cut out promptly

Clip back heathers like this *Erica carnea* 'Aurea' after flowering but don't cut too far into the old wood

Drimys Winter's bark

Size if unpruned: *Drimys winteri* will reach 2 x 2m (6½ x 6½ft) after five years, and 4 x 4m (13 x 13ft) after 20 years.
Pruning: None essential but old and misshapen plants may be pruned fairly hard immediately after flowering to restore their shape (page 18).

Elaeagnus

Size if unpruned: Most garden varieties will reach about 1.2 x 1.2m (4 x 4ft) after five years and 3 x 3m (10 x 10ft) after 20 years.
Pruning: None essential, but if necessary to tidy or cut back mature specimens, prune deciduous varieties in early spring and evergreens such as *Elaeagnus pungens* 'Maculata' and *E. x ebbingei* 'Limelight' in mid-spring. If shoots bearing pure green leaves appear on variegated forms they should be cut out immediately (page 13)

Enkianthus

Size if unpruned: *Enkianthus campanulatus* and *E. perulatus* will reach about 1.5 x 1m (5 x 3ft) after five years and 3 x 3m (10 x 10ft) after 20 years; *E. cernuus* about two-thirds of this size.
Pruning: None essential, though the plants will withstand being cut back into old wood in spring if necessary to restore shape or rejuvenate old specimens.

Erica Heather, Heath

Size if unpruned: Varieties of *Erica carnea* will mostly reach 15 x 80cm (6 x 32in) after about five years; *E. x darleyensis* varieties will reach 30cm-1m x 1m (12in-3ft x 3ft); *E. cinerea* varieties about 30 x 45-60cm (12 x 18-24in).
Pruning: Cut off dead flowers in spring, using shears (page 20); do not cut too close to the old wood. Heathers become straggly in time and will generally need replacing after eight or nine years.

Escallonia

Size if unpruned: Up to 2 x 2m (6½ x 6½ft) after five years, and about 4 x 4m (13 x 13ft) after 20 years.
Pruning: None essential if grown informally, apart from removing any frost-damaged shoots in spring. Mature plants will benefit from having the oldest one-third of all shoots cut back in spring (page 23). For hedges see page 63.

Eucalyptus Gum tree

Size if unpruned: About 5 x 2m (16 x 6½ft) after five years, 20 x 8m (65 x 25ft) after 20 years.
Pruning: None essential, but they will then make large trees and be prone to damage in hard winters or strong winds. It is better to cut them back hard or by 'stooling' them (page 23) every spring or every other spring to make a multi-stemmed shrub with prolific and attractive juvenile foliage.

The attractive juvenile foliage on *Eucalyptus gunnii divaricata* is produced as a response to hard annual pruning

Eucryphia

Size if unpruned: *Eucryphia* x *nymansensis* 'Nymansay' will reach 2 x 1m (6½ x 3ft) after five years; 8 x 4m (25 x 13ft) after 20 years.

But they must have good growing conditions to achieve this; an acid soil is ideal.
Pruning: None essential, but young plants may be encouraged to bush out by pinching out leading shoots.

Euonymus

Size if unpruned: *Euonymus alatus* will reach about 1 x 1m (3 x 3ft) after five years and 2 x 4m (6½ x 13ft) after 20 years; *E. europaeus* about 2 x 2m (6½ x 6½ft) after five years and 4 x 6m (13 x 20ft) after 20 years; *E. fortunei* will reach its maximum height of about 60cm (24in) and a spread of about 1m (3ft) after five years, eventually spreading to 3m (10ft).
Pruning: None essential, but any all-green shoots that appear on variegated forms should be removed at once (page 13). Most species will tolerate being cut back moderately hard in mid-spring if necessary to restore shape.

Fagus Beech

Size if unpruned: The popular Weeping Beech *Fagus sylvatica pendula* will eventually reach about 15 x 20m (50 x 65ft); normal upright forms will reach about 3 x 3m (10 x 10ft) after five years, 14 x 14m (45 x 45ft) after 20 years, and continue growing to about 25 x 16m (80 x 55ft) after 50 years.
Pruning: None essential, but plants grown as specimen trees will tolerate the removal of branches. Care must be taken, however, not to leave any branch stubs as they are a magnet for coral spot disease (page 15). See also hedges page 64.

Fallopia Russian vine, Mile-a-minute vine

Size if unpruned: About 5m (16ft) after three years; up to 20m (65ft) after 10 years.
Pruning: None essential, but *Fallopia baldschuanica* may be cut very hard back in spring, if required, to limit its size. If it is routinely pruned extremely hard, it would be more widely accepted for the attractive plant that it is.

TREES, SHRUBS AND·CLIMBERS

Fatsia japonica and x Fatshedera lizei

Size if unpruned: *Fatsia japonica* will reach 4 x 4m (13 x 13ft) after 15 years, its relative x *Fatshedera lizei*, (a cross with *Hedera helix*) will attain about 2-5 x 3m (6½-16 x 10ft).

Pruning: None essential but prone to winter cold damage and so damaged shoots should be cut back in spring to the first healthy stem.

Forsythia

Size if unpruned: Most varieties including the popular forms of *Forsythia x intermedia* such as 'Lynwood' and 'Spectabilis' will reach 2.5 x 1.5m (8 x 5ft) after five years, and 4 x 3.5m (13 x 11ft) after 20 years; *F. suspensa* is more spreading, and will eventually reach 3 x 4-5m (10 x 13-16ft).

Forsythia x intermedia **is best when pruned every two or three years immediately after flowering**

Pruning: Every two or three years, immediately after flowering, remove the oldest one-third of the flowering shoots to soil level, or to the lowest strong, young shoot (page 23). Remove any over-crowded shoots at the same time. Neglected plants may be rejuvenated by cutting back completely to soil level, but will not flower fully for two or three years. Plants trained against a wall (as *F. suspensa* often is) should be cut hard back, cutting up to 5cm (2in) into the old wood immediately after flowering (page 21). For hedges see page 62.

Fothergilla

Size if unpruned: *Fothergilla major* will attain about 2.5 x 2m (8 x 6½ft) after 10-15 years.

Pruning: None essential but damaged branches should be removed in spring

Fraxinus Ash

Size if unpruned: Most normal species of *Fraxinus* including the native *F. excelsior* will reach about 6 x 2m (20 x 6½ft) after five years, 20 x 7m (65 x 23ft) after 20 years, and continue growing to about 24 x 10m (75 x 33ft) after 50 years; but *F. ornus* will reach only about two-thirds of this size, and the weeping *F. excelsior* 'Pendula' (the best garden variety) will reach about 10 x 10m (33 x 33ft) eventually.

Pruning: None essential and specimen trees will look unsightly if pruned although damaged branches may safely be cut back to the trunk in the usual way (page 25). *F. excelsior* 'Pendula' should have any upright shoots cut out to maintain an attractive shape.

Fremontodendron

Size if unpruned: The popular hybrid 'California Glory' will attain about 3 x 3m (10 x 10ft) after five years, and 6 x 6m (20 x 20ft) after 20 years although they are not naturally long-lived plants and may die suddenly for no evident reason.

Pruning: None essential, apart from removing frost-damaged shoots. If trained against a wall the plant may be spur-pruned (page 7) by cutting back the side shoots after flowering to about 4cm (1½in) from their bases.

Fuchsia

Size if unpruned: Ranges widely from 50 x 50cm (20 x 20in) for dwarf varieties to a maximum of 2 x 2m (6½ x 6½ft) after 10 years for upright, hardy varieties.

Pruning: In mild areas, none essential. If frost damage occurs, cut back in spring to at least 15cm (6in) below damaged shoots, or to soil level (page 22). Old and woody specimens may be rejuvenated by similarly cutting hard back in spring. Never prune in autumn even if the

Fremontodendron will flower most profusely and neatly against a wall when spur-pruned

shoots are killed by late frosts as the dead shoots are needed for winter protection. For hedges see page 65.

Garrya Tassel bush

Size if unpruned: *Garrya elliptica* will attain 3 x 2m (10 x 6½ft) after five years, and 5 x 4m (16 x 13ft) after 20 years.
Pruning: None essential, but if growing in a confined space may have previous season's shoots cut back to 10cm (4in) above their base immediately after flowering. Garryas are prone to coral spot disease and so care should be taken to leave no branch stubs.

Genista Broom

Size if unpruned: *Genista lydia* will reach about 50cm x 1.2m (20 in x 4ft) after five years and 1 x 3m (3 x 10ft) after 20 years. The largest species, *G. aetnensis*, forms a small tree, reaching about 5 x 5m (16 x 16ft) eventually.
Pruning: I am not enthusiastic about pruning genistas as I find they respond by dying back although some gardeners trim back the dead flower stems as the flowers fade.

Gleditsia Honey locust

Size if unpruned: *Gleditsia triacanthos* may reach a height of 30m (100ft) in favourably mild areas eventually; but the commoner and more popular golden-foliaged form 'Sunburst' will reach only about 2.5 x 1.3m (8 x 4½ft) after five years and 6 x 5m (20 x 16ft) after 20 years.
Pruning: None essential, but young trees may have the previous season's growth shortened in spring to improve their shape.

Griselinia

Size if unpruned: *Griselinia littoralis* will reach 6 x 5m (20 x 16ft).
Pruning: None essential although shoots damaged by winter cold may be cut back to the main stems in spring. For hedges see page 63.

Hamamelis Witch hazel

Size if unpruned: The commonest species, including *Hamamelis mollis* and *H.* x *intermedia* will attain about 1.5 x 1.5m (5 x 5ft) after five years, and 5 x 4m (16 x 13ft) after 20 years.
Pruning: None essential and rather like magnolias, witch hazels respond badly to pruning by displaying die-back and/or proliferation of small twiggy shoots.

Ficus Ornamental fig

Size if unpruned: The commonest species, *Ficus pumila*, or creeping fig will attain about 1m (3ft) after three years; up to 4-5m (13-16ft) eventually.
Pruning: None essential, but straggly or stray shoots may be clipped back to the main stem in spring to improve shape.

For Fruiting Figs see page 88

Delay the pruning of hardy fuchsias like *Fuchsia magellanica* 'Versicolor' until spring to give them frost protection over winter

Hebe

Size if unpruned: The low-growing forms such as *Hebe* 'Pewter Dome' and *H. pinguifolia* 'Pagei' will reach about 30 x 80cm (12 x 32in) after five years and 50cm x 1m (20in x 3ft) after 20 years; taller varieties like the popular 'Autumn Glory' will reach about 1 x 1m (3 x 3ft) after five years and 1.2 x 3m (4 x 10ft) after 20 years.

Pruning: Normal-leaved varieties may be lightly trimmed in spring to encourage new shoots although those such as *H. rakaiensis* which naturally form a neat dome and also those like *H. cupressoides* and *H. ochracea* with conifer-like foliage are best not pruned.

Hedera Ivy

Size if unpruned: The most vigorous ivies like *Hedera algeriensis* 'Gloire de Marengo' may reach up to 15m (50ft) in 10 years, the least vigorous forms of *H. helix* barely attain 1m (3ft).

Pruning: None essential, but if necessary to limit size may be cut back with secateurs or shears in spring. Try to avoid cutting into wood older than four or five years as it regenerates very slowly and try not to use shears on those forms with large leaves which will turn brown and become unsightly in consequence. Cut out all-green shoots on variegated varieties (page 13).

Helichrysum

Size if unpruned: The alpine species such as *Helichrysum coralloides* will reach about 25 x 15cm (10 x 6in); among the common shrubby species, *H. splendidum* will reach 1.2 x 1.2m (4 x 4ft) while the popular, tender, silver-leaved trailing shrub *H. petiolare* will, in time, form mounds about 40cm x 1.5m (16in x 5ft), although it is often grown as an annual.

Hibiscus syriacus **'Red Heart' will flower more profusely with annual spring pruning**

Pruning: *H. splendidum* may be cut hard back each spring into the previous year's wood (page 18); other shrubby species may be trimmed lightly after flowering. The alpine types are best left alone.

Hibiscus

Size if unpruned: All hardy *Hibiscus* are forms of *H. syriacus* and attain about 1 x 1m (3 x 3ft) after five years and 3-4 x 3-4m (10-13 x 10-13ft) in favourable conditions after 20 years.

Pruning: None essential; to encourage bushier growth on mature plants the previous season's shoots may be cut back by up to half in spring (page 18).

Hippophae Sea buckthorn

Size if unpruned: The commonest species, the native *Hippophae rhamnoides* will attain about 4 x 4m (13 x 13ft) after 10 years.

Pruning: None essential but shoots damaged by winter cold (as they tend to be in inland gardens) should be cut back to the main stems in spring.

Holboellia

Size if unpruned: The evergreen, twining climber *Holboellia coriacea* will attain 2m (6½ft) after three

years, and 8m (25ft) eventually.
Pruning: None essential, but may be trimmed lightly to shape in spring if space is limited.

Humulus Hop

Size if unpruned: Once established, the golden-foliaged *Humulus lupulus* 'Aureus' will reach 7m (23ft) in a season.
Pruning: None required while growing, but in late autumn cut back to about 30cm (12in) above soil level, then back to soil level in spring (page 22).

Hydrangea

Size if unpruned: *Hydrangea macrophylla*, *H. arborescens* and *H. quercifolia* will reach about 1 x 1m (3 x 3ft) after five years and 2-3 x 2-3m (6½-10 x 6½-10ft) after 20 years. *H. paniculata*, including its beautiful variety 'Grandiflora' is faster-growing and will reach about 2 x 2m (6½2 x 6½2ft) after five years and 4 x 4m (13 x 13ft) after 20 years.
Pruning: Most forms require none, but *H. paniculata* may be pruned in mid-spring by cutting back the previous season's growth to within three buds of the base

Hydrangea macrophylla varieties will be bushier and neater if they are pruned fairly hard in spring

(page 18), and established specimens of the popular mop-head varieties of *H. macrophylla* should have all dead flowerheads cut back in late spring to a strong pair of new leaves, and up to one-third of the oldest or weakest shoots cut down at the same time to just above soil level (page 23). Do not prune in autumn as the dead shoots provide essential winter protection.

Hydrangea (climbing) /Schizophragma /Pileostegia

Size if unpruned: *Hydrangea petiolaris* is slow to establish, reaching only about 1.8 x 1.8m (6 x 6ft) after five years, but may then reach up to 12 x 12m (40 x 40ft) after 20 years. *Schizophragma integrifolium* and *Pileostegia viburnoides* will reach about half this size eventually.
Pruning: None essential and best left unpruned but if space is limited side-shoots may be may be cut back to the main stem in spring.

Hypericum St John's wort

Size if unpruned: Most shrubby forms of *Hypericum* will grow fairly slowly to reach about 50-80 x 50-80cm (20-32 x 20-32in) after five years and 1-1.2 x 1-1.2m (3-4 x 3-4ft) after 20 years; *H. calycinum* has a maximum height of 45cm (18in) and will spread to 1m (3ft) after five years, 2m (6½ft) after 20 years.
Pruning: Varieties like 'Hidcote' which are grown for their flowers or fruit should be pruned every spring by cutting back the oldest one-third of shoots to soil level (page 23). Those grown for their foliage should be cut back to soil level in spring every other year. This is also true of *H. calycinum* if appearance is important although where grown in wilder places as ground cover, it may be left unpruned.

Itea Sweetspire

Size if unpruned: The lovely and underrated evergreen *Itea ilicifolia* will attain about 3 x 3m (10 x 10ft) eventually
Pruning: None essential but dead or damaged shoots may be cut back to the nearest main stem.

Jasminum Jasmine

Size if unpruned: Winter-flowering *Jasminum nudiflorum* will attain 1.5 x 1.5m (5 x 5ft) after five years, 3 x 3m (10 x 10ft) after 20 years. The summer-flowering *J. officinale* will reach about 2.5 x 2.5m (8 x 8ft) after five years and 9 x 9m (30 x 30ft) after 20 years; *J. x stephanense* will reach about 1.8 x 1.8m (6 x 6ft) after five years and 4.5 x 4.5m 15 x 15ft) after 20 years.
Pruning: Cut back the oldest one-third of the stems of the summer-flowering jasmines to soil level every spring (page 23). *J. nudiflorum* may be treated similarly or the dead flower shoots and any frost-damaged shoots may be cut back to new wood after flowering. Alternatively, if grown against a wall or as a hedge, winter jasmine may be clipped to shape with shears after flowering (page 20).

The vigour of *Jasminum nudiflorum* will be maintained best with selective spring pruning

Juniperus Juniper

Size if unpruned: *Juniperus communis* in its native form will reach about 3 x 2m (10 x 6½ft); its variety 'Compressa' about 75 x 25cm (30 x 10in) and 'Hibernica' about 4m x 30cm (13ft x 12in); among other popular forms, *J. scopulorum* 'Skyrocket' is about 8m x 75cm (25ft x 30in); *J. squamata* 'Blue Star' is about 50 x 60cm (20 x 24in).
Pruning: None essential but odd wayward shoots may be clipped out between spring and autumn.

The occasional upright shoots on prostrate varieties of junipers should be cut out promptly

Kalmia Calico bush

Size if unpruned: *Kalmia latifolia* will attain 1.5 x 1.5m (5 x 5ft) after five years, and 3 x 3m (10 x 10ft) after 20 years.
Pruning: None essential but any damaged shoots may be cut back to the main stems in spring.

Kerria Jew's mallow

Size if unpruned: The only species, *Kerria japonica* will attain 3 x 1.5m (10 x 5ft) after five years, and 3 x 3.5m (10 x 11ft) after 20 years.
Pruning: Cut back the oldest one-third of the shoots to soil level immediately after flowering (page 23).

This *Kerria japonica* 'Pleniflora' requires thinning out; if the oldest shoots are removed each spring, this congestion and diminished vigour will be avoided

Laburnum

Size if unpruned: *Laburnum alpinum* 'Pendulum' will reach only about 3 x 1.5m (10 x 5ft) eventually, unless grafted, as it often is, on to 1.5m (5ft) or 2.5m (8ft) stems. The best garden variety with very long inflorescences is *L.* x *watereri* 'Vossii' which will reach 4 x 2m (13 x 6½ft) after five years and 7 x 4m (23 x 13ft) after 20 years. This variety may be trained as a climber but even then should be pruned as little as possible.

Pruning: None essential, and should be avoided unless the plants are damaged. Laburnums don't usually live for much more than about 25 years, and their decline is hastened by decay fungi that enter readily through cut branch surfaces.

Lapageria rosea Chilean bellflower

Size if unpruned: The only species and its popular varieties 'Albiflora' and 'Nash Court' will attain 2 x 2m (6½ x 6½ft) after five years, and 6.5 x 6.5m (22 x 22ft) after 20 years.

Pruning: None essential, but if necessary to remove frost-damaged or congested shoots it should be done in spring, cutting back to a strong bud or the junction with the parent stem.

Larix (and Pseudolarix) Larch

Size if unpruned: Most species will attain about 30 x 8m (100 x 25ft).

Pruning: Any lateral shoots competing with the central leader on young trees should be removed as soon as possible (page 60). The lowest branches may also be removed to leave a clear trunk to enhance the appearance of specimen trees (page 13).

Laurus nobilis Sweet bay

Size if unpruned: Will attain about 12 x 10m (40 x 33ft).

Pruning: None essential if grown informally, but there will be considerable leaf and branch death in cold winters and this may be cut back very hard in spring (page 18); the plant will re-grow from

very old wood. May also be trimmed to shape in mid-spring. For hedges and topiary see page 63 and page 66.

Lavandula Lavender

Size if unpruned: *Lavandula angustifolia* will reach about 1 x 1m (3 x 3ft) after five years; the other forms mentioned here are more compact and will reach no more than 50 x 60cm (20 x 24in) in the same time; dwarf varieties even less. Lavender plants tend to become very woody with age and may need replacing after six or seven years.

Pruning: None essential; to encourage neat, bushy growth trim the plants lightly in mid-spring and then prune hard after the flowers have faded, just cutting into the woody growth at the base of the flower stems (page 20). If using the flowers for pot pourri, cut them just as they open fully. For hedges see page 65.

Lavenders like the popular *Lavandula angustifolia* 'Hidcote' look bare and twiggy after pruning but tiny new green leaves soon begin to appear

Leucothoe

Size if unpruned: *Leucothoe fontanesiana* and its variegated form 'Rainbow' will attain about 1.5 x 3m (5 x 10ft).

Pruning: None essential, but to promote new growth on mature plants cut the oldest one-third of the shoots down to ground level in spring (page 23).

Leycesteria Himalayan Honeysuckle

Size if unpruned: The form most widely cultivated, *Leycesteria formosa* will reach 2.5 x 2.5m (8 x 8ft) after five years, and 2.5 x 3.5m (8 x 11ft) after 20 years.

Pruning: Cut back all shoots to a few centimetres above soil level in early spring (page 22).

Ligustrum Privet

Size if unpruned: The best hedging variety, *Ligustrum ovalifolium* will eventually reach 6 x 6m (20 x 20ft); *L. lucidum* about 8 x 8m (25 x 25ft).

Pruning: None essential, but the plants will tolerate being cut back hard, which is why they are so popular as hedges. For hedges see page 63.

Liriodendron Tulip tree

Size if unpruned: *Liriodendron tulipifera* will reach about 3.5 x 2m (11 x 6½ft) after five years, and 14 x 8m (45 x 25ft) after 20 years, and will carry on growing for up to 50 years, reaching an eventual height of 30m (100ft). The beautiful form 'Aureomarginata' with golden leaf edges will reach only about two-thirds of this size.

Pruning: None essential and decay fungi may enter if branches are removed. The trees are naturally very slow to flower (you may have to wait for 20 years) and pruning will not alter this.

Lonicera Honeysuckle

Size if unpruned: The deciduous *Lonicera fragrantissima* will reach 1.2 x 2m (4 x 6½ft) after five years; the popular small-leaved evergreen *L. nitida* 'Baggesen's Gold' about 60cm x 1.3m (24in x 4½ft) in the same time.
Pruning: None essential, but the deciduous shrubby species may be trimmed after flowering. For hedges see page 63.

I believe that honeysuckles look best when allowed fairly free rein to grow over trees

Lonicera Climbing honeysuckle

Size if unpruned: Most of the popular garden forms will reach about 2m (6½ft) after three years although some are rather more vigorous: *Lonicera japonica* will then reach about 9m (30ft) after 20 years, *L. brownii* and *L. periclymenum* in its many popular varieties, about 6m (20ft), and *L. x tellmaniana* about 4.5m (15ft).
Pruning: I find there are two different ways of growing and pruning climbing honeysuckles: either they may be left to their own devices, to form a natural and rather untidy tangle; or they may have one-third of all shoots cut back to soil level each spring (page 23).

Magnolia

Size if unpruned: The evergreen *Magnolia grandiflora* will reach 3 x 1m (10 x 3ft) after five years and 8 x 4m (25 x 13ft) after 20 years; among the more familiar deciduous forms, *M. kobus*, *M. x loebneri* and *M. soulangeana* will reach about 4 x 2m (13 x 6½ft) after five years and 9 x 8m (30 x 25ft) after 20 years; *M. liliiflora* will reach about 1.5 x 1.5m (5 x 5ft) after five years and 4 x 4m (13 x 13ft) after 20 years.
Pruning: None essential, but lower branches may be removed to encourage a more tree-like shape. If *M. grandiflora* is trained against a wall, it will also be necessary to remove some branches to shape the plant. Prune deciduous species in summer, and evergreens in mid-spring but, overall, prune magnolias as little as possible and then, if you must, remove whole branches. Trimming and snipping leads to a proliferation of thin twiggy shoots.

Mahonia

Size if unpruned: The Oregon grape, *Mahonia aquifolium* will reach its maximum height of about 1-1.2m (3-4ft) after three or four years and will then spread to about 3m (10ft) eventually. The upright species, such as *M. japonica*, will reach about 1.5 x 2m (5-6½ft) after five years and 3-4 x 3m (10-13 x 10ft) after 20 years; some of the hybrids like *M. x media*

Given space, the large forms of *Mahonia* such as 'Winter Sun' are best left unpruned

'Charity' may eventually reach 5m (16ft).
Pruning: None essential for *M. aquifolium* if grown informally, though mature plants may be rejuvenated by cutting up to half of the old woody stems to soil level every 3 or 4 years (page 23). This species may sucker extensively and these should be removed if it is not wanted as ground cover. For *M. x media* 'Charity', *M. japonica* and related forms, non-flowering shoots may be cut back by about half in mid-spring if a more compact shape is required.

Malus Crab apple

Size if unpruned: *Malus floribunda* will reach about 4 x 1.5m (13 x 5ft) after five years and 8 x 6m (25 x 20ft) after 20 years; *M. hupehensis* and *M. transitoria* will reach about two-thirds of this size. Among smaller types, *M. sargentii* will reach about 4 x 5m (13 x 16ft) after 20 years; *M. sieboldii* about 3 x 3m (10 x 10ft). All of these species however, as well as named varieties such as 'Golden Hornet', are obtainable grafted on to size limiting apple rootstocks.
Pruning: None essential, but any damaged or misplaced branches may be removed during the winter. See also apples page 75.

Myrtus Myrtle

Size if unpruned: *Myrtus communis* will reach 1 x 1m (3 x 3ft) after five years.
Pruning: None essential, but untidy shoots may be cut out at the base in mid-spring.

Nandina Sacred bamboo

Size if unpruned: The only species, *Nandina domestica*, will attain 50 x 80cm (20 x 32in) after five years, 1 x 1.2m (3 x 4ft) after 20 years.

Pruning: None essential, but it is sensible to cut away dead flowering or fruiting stems, and to cut out very old stems at the base in spring.

Osmanthus

Size if unpruned: *Osmanthus x burkwoodii* will reach 2 x 2m (6½ x6½ft) after five years; *O. delavayi* and *O. heterophyllus* 'Variegatus' about 1.3 x 1.3m (4½ x 4½ft).
Pruning: Normally none needed but old, misplaced shoots may be cut out in spring. Old, poorly shaped bushes will re-generate if cut back in spring (page 18).

Ozothamnus

Size if unpruned: *Ozothamnus ledifolius* will reach about 1 x 1m (3 x 3ft); *O. rosmarinifolius* about 2 x 1.5m (6½ x 5ft).
Pruning: Normally none needed although frost damaged shoots should be cut out in spring, cutting as little as possible into old wood.

Parrotia

Size if unpruned: The only species *Parrotia persica*, will attain about 2.5 x 2m (8 x 6½ft) after five years and 10 x 8m (30 x 25ft) after 20 years.
Pruning: None essential, but may be shaped in spring if preferred as a shrub rather than a tree.

Parthenocissus

Size if unpruned: Among the commonest species, *Parthenocissus quinquefolia* will reach about 9 x 9m (30 x 30ft) eventually; and the beautiful large leaved *P. henryana* about 6 x 6m (20 x 20ft). *P. tricuspidata* is the most vigorous and will reach about 2.5 x 2.5m (8 x 8ft) after five years and 10 x 10m (33 x 33ft) after 20 years.

Pruning: None essential, though when the plants are young it is wise to pinch out some shoots to encourage branching. Once they are established it is important to keep them clear of window frames and roof tiles by running an old knife along the shoots once or twice a year about 15-20cm (6-8ft) away from the limit.

Passiflora Passion flower

Size if unpruned: The only reliably hardy species, *Passiflora caerulea* will reach about 2.5 x 2.5m (8 x 8ft) after five years, and 20 x 20ft after 20 years.
Pruning: Any frost-damaged shoots should be removed in spring. In mild areas it should be possible to maintain a permanent framework of strong shoots; but in colder areas it may be necessary to cut back more or less to soil level after the winter (page 22).

The pruning of *Passiflora caerulea* will almost certainly need to be harder in cold areas

Periploca Silk vine

Size if unpruned: *Periploca graeca* will reach about 2m (6½ft) after three years; 9m (30ft) eventually.
Pruning: None essential, though if necessary to rejuvenate overgrown plants, they may be cut hard fairly back in the spring (page 18).

Phillyrea

Size if unpruned: *Phillyrea angustifolia* will reach about 1.2 x 1.2m (4 x 4ft) after five years and 3 x 3m (10 x 10ft) eventually; *P. latifolia* slightly less than this.
Pruning: None essential if grown as individual shrubs although damaged or misplaced branches may be cut out in spring, cutting just slightly into old wood. For hedges see page 65.

Photinia

Size if unpruned: The beautiful evergreen *Photinia x fraseri* 'Red Robin' will reach 1.5 x 2m (5 x 6½ft) after five years and eventually 5 x 4m (16 x 13ft).
Pruning: None essential if grown informally, but the appeal of *P. x fraseri* is the bright red young growth and it is best lightly trimmed in summer to promote this. For hedges see page 65.

Physocarpus Nine bark

Size if unpruned: The popular golden-foliaged *Physocarpus opulifolius* 'Dart's Gold' will reach about 1-1.5 x 1-1.5m (3-5 x 3-5ft) after five years.
Pruning: Cut back approximately the oldest one third of the shoots to soil level on mature plants after flowering to encourage new growth (page 23).

Picea Spruce

Size if unpruned: Most specimen spruces, including the beautiful and popular *Picea breweriana*, may eventually reach about 30 x 5-7m (100 x 16-23ft).
Pruning: Any lateral shoots competing with the central leader on young trees should be removed as early as possible. But this aside, spruces, like most specimen conifers are best left alone.

Pieris

Size if unpruned: The two most popular varieties, *Pieris floribunda* 'Forest Flame' and *P. japonica* 'Variegata' will attain about 80cm x 1m (32in x 3ft) after five years, reaching 2 x 4m (6½ x 13ft) eventually.
Pruning: None essential, but any damaged shoots should be removed in late spring, cutting back to the main stem.

Pieris **'Forest Flame' will produce attractive new shoots and flowers with little need for pruning**

Pinus Pine

Size if unpruned: Although there are several popular dwarf forms, among the best tree sized pines for large gardens are *Pinus cembra* and *P. heldreichii* var. *leucodermis* which will eventually reach about 15 x 5m (50 x 16ft), *P. nigra* ssp. *laricio* which reaches about 30 x 8m (100 x 25ft), *P. radiata* about 20 x 10m (65 x 33ft) and the native *P. sylvestris* about 25 x 10m (80 x 33ft).
Pruning: Any lateral shoots competing with the central leader on young trees should be removed as early as possible. But this aside, pines like most specimen conifers are best left alone.

Pittosporum

Size if unpruned: The most popular foliage varieties such as *Pittosporum eugenioides* 'Garnettii' and *P. tenuifolium* will reach about 1.5-2 x 1m (5-6½ x 3ft) in mild conditions after five years, and about 6 x 2.5-3m (20 x 8-10ft) after 20 years.
Pruning: None essential if grown informally, but any broken or winter-damaged shoots should be pruned in mid-spring. For hedges see page 63.

Populus Poplar

Size if unpruned: *Populus lasiocarpa* and *P. tremula* will reach about 2 x 1m (6½ x 3ft) after five years, 8 x 4m (25 x 13ft) after 20 years, and continue growing to about 10 x 8m (33 x 25ft) after 50 years. *P. nigra italica* will reach about 5 x 1m (16 x 3ft) after five years, 20 x 4m (65 x 13ft) after 20 years, and 25 x 5m (80 x 16ft) after 50 years. Most other forms will reach 5 x 4m (16 x 13ft) after five years, 20 x 10m (65 x 33ft) after 20 years, and 25 x 15m (80 x 50 ft) after 50 years.
Pruning: None essential but in small gardens, most poplars will soon outgrow

Winter flowering *Prunus subhirtella* 'Autumnalis' always contain a great many dead twigs which should be cut out

their space. Varieties with golden or variegated foliage are best pollarded or cut hard back each or every other year to maximise foliage effect (page 24). Any pruning on poplars is best done in early winter to prevent 'bleeding'.

Potentilla

Size if unpruned: The more vigorous varieties like 'Daydawn and 'Elizabeth' will reach their ultimate size of about 1.2 x 1.2m (4 x 4ft) after eight or nine years; the less vigorous forms will not generally exceed about 60 x 60cm (24 x 24in) eventually.

Pruning: None essential, but most varieties will benefit having the oldest one-third of their shoots cut back to just above soil level each spring (page 23).

Prunus
Plums, Cherries, Laurels

Size if unpruned: Among popular blossom cherries, *Prunus sargentii* will reach 3.5 x 2.5m (11 x 8ft) after five years, 9 x 10m (30 x 33ft) after 20 years;

P. serrula: 4 x 2m (14 x 6½ft) after five years, 7 x 4m (13 x 13ft) after 20 years; *P.* 'Spire': 3.5 x 2m (11 x 6½ft) after five years, 9 x 3 (30 x 10ft) after 20 years; *P. subhirtella* 'Autumnalis': 1.5 x 2m (5 x 6½ft) after five years, 7 x 7m (23 x 23ft) after 20 years; *P.* 'Tai-haku': 3.5 x 2.5m (11 x 8ft) after five years, 8 x 8m (25 x 25ft) after 20 years; *P. yedoensis*: 3.5 x 2.5m (11 x 8ft) after five years, 9 x 7m (30 x 23ft) after 20 years. Among evergreen foliage varieties, *P. laurocerasus* will reach 3 x 3m (10 x 10ft) after five years and eventually 8-10 x 8m (20-33 x 25ft), although the popular variety 'Otto Luyken' will reach only 1.5 x 1.5m (5 x 5ft); *P. lusitanica* will reach about 1 x 1m (3 x 3ft) in five years and 5 x 5m (16 x 16ft) eventually.

Pruning: None essential in spring-blossoming varieties, but any damaged or unwanted branches may be removed in late spring. *P. subhirtella* 'Autumnalis' is prone to extensive twig death in winter and these twigs are best removed in spring just before the leaves open. No pruning is needed on the evergreen varieties. For hedges see page 63.

Pseudotsuga
Douglas fir

Size if unpruned: *Pseudotsuga menziesii* will eventually attain 25 x 12m (80 x 40ft).
Pruning: Any lateral shoots competing with the central leader on young trees should be removed as early as possible. But this aside, Douglas firs, like most specimen conifers are best left alone.

Pyracantha Firethorn

Size if unpruned: Most common varieties will attain about 2 x 1.5m (6½ x 5ft) after five years, 4 x 3-4m (13 x 10-13ft) after 20 years.
Pruning: If grown free-standing, none is essential apart from occasional shaping in spring. When grown against a wall, prune in spring after flowering, removing side-shoots to within 2cm (¾in) of their base to produce a plant either formally trained to a neat geometric shape or less formally as a simple two-dimensional shrub. Some loss of fruit will of course be inevitable. See also hedges page 64.

With careful annual pruning, a *Pyracantha* can be trained to precise geometric patterns

If size permits, pull away dead *Rhododendron* flower heads by hand

Pyrus Pear

Size if unpruned: The most popular forms including the willow-leaved pear *Pyrus salicifolia* 'Pendula' and *P. calleryana* 'Chanticleer' will attain 3 x 2m (10 x 6½ft) after five years, and 8 x 6m (25 x 20ft) after 20 years.
Pruning: Apart from the removal of damaged or diseased branches during spring, ornamental pears are best left unpruned.

Quercus Oak

Size if unpruned: Most oaks, deciduous and evergreen, are slow growing and will reach about 3 x 2.5m (10 x 8ft) after five years, 12 x 8m (40 x 25ft) after 20 years, but may then continue growing, depending on conditions, to reach as much as 25 x 18m (80 x 60ft). *Quercus cerris* the Turkey Oak may grow even larger than this although *Q. phellos* the Willow Oak reaches about one-third less.
Pruning: Oaks require no pruning other than the removal of damaged branches which is best done in mid-spring (page 25)

Rhamnus Buckthorn

Size if unpruned: The native *Rhamnus cathartica* and the popular ornamental *R. alaternus* 'Argenteovariegata' will attain about 2 x 1.5m (6½ x 5ft) after five years, and 5 x 4m (16 x 13ft) after 20 years.
Pruning: None essential, but evergreen forms may be trimmed to shape in spring. See also hedges page 63.

Rhodochiton Purple bell vine, Parachute plant

Size if unpruned: The only species, *Rhodochiton atrosanguineus*, in favourable conditions will reach about 3m (10ft) in one season.
Pruning: If grown as a perennial outdoors, the above-ground growth will die back in winter and should be trimmed away to soil level in autumn and the crown of the plant then protected.

Rhododendron (including *Azalea*)

Size if unpruned: Rhododendrons: large-flowered hybrids will reach 1.2 x 1.5m (4 x 5ft) after five years and 3 x 4m (10 x 13ft) after 20 years; dwarf hybrids and low-growing species reach 60 x 60cm (24 x 24in) after five years and 1 x 1.5m (3 x 5ft) after 20 years. Azaleas: dwarf evergreen forms: 60 x 60cm (24 x 24in) after five years and 1 x 1.2m (3 x 4ft) after 20 years; tall-growing deciduous forms:

If *Rhus typhina* is pruned back to soil level, more of the attractive foliage will be produced

1 x 1m (3 x 3ft) after five years and 2.3 x 2.7m (7½ x 9ft) after 20 years.
Pruning: None essential, but where practicable the dead flowerheads should be pulled away, taking care not to harm the new flower buds at their base. This improves the appearance of the plant and helps to encourage further blooming. Damaged or misplaced branches should be cut back to the parent stem in spring.

Rhus Sumac

Size if unpruned: The stagshorn sumac, *Rhus typhina*, and the cut-leaved *Rhus glabra* 'Laciniata' will reach about 2 x 2m (6½ x 6½ft) after five years and 6-7 x 5m (20-23 x 16ft) after 20 years.
Pruning: There are two ways of growing sumacs: either don't prune and allow the plants to reach their full size (and stark winter appearance), or cut them back to ground level each spring to encourage the growth of new shoots with larger leaves (page 22).

Ribes Ornamental currant

Size if unpruned: Most forms will reach 1.5 x 1.5m (5 x 5ft) after five years and 2.5 x 2.5m (8 x 8ft) after 20 years.
Pruning: *Ribes odoratum* and varieties of *R. sanguineum* such as the popular 'Brocklebankii' and 'Pulborough Scarlet' should have the oldest one-third of all shoots cut out in spring, after flowering, to prevent the plants becoming leggy (page 23). *R. speciosum* needs only to have frost-damaged shoots removed after the winter. See also hedges page 64.

Robinia

Size if unpruned: *Robinia hispida* will reach 2 x 2m (6½ x 6½ft) after five years and 6 x 6m (20 x 20ft) after 20 years; *R. pseudoacacia* will reach about 3 x 2.5m

(10 x 8ft) after five years and 16 x 11m (55 x 36ft) after 20 years; 'Frisia' will reach about 12 x 6m (40 x 20ft) eventually.
Pruning: None essential, but the branches are brittle and some winter damage may be expected. This should be cut back to healthy wood in spring. As an alternative to growing *R. pseudoacacia* as a tree, it may be pollarded or stooled by cutting back all branches to just above soil-level in mid-spring (page 22).

Rosmarinus Rosemary

Size if unpruned: Most varieties of the three common species will reach their ultimate size of about 1.5 x 1.5m (5 x 5ft) after five or seven years, but 'Miss Jessopp's Upright' is slightly more vigorous while 'Severn Sea' will reach only 1 x 1m (3 x 3ft).
Pruning: Rosemaries soon become leggy and the best plan for free-standing ornamental or culinary plants is to cut out the oldest one-third of the shoots to just above soil level every year (page 22). But they do respond well to being clipped and this may be done to a neat shape in early summer. See also hedges page 64.

Rubus

Size if unpruned: Among the upright forms, *Rubus* 'Benenden' will reach about 1 x 1m (3 x 3ft) after five years and 3 x 3m (10 x 10ft) after 15 years; *Rubus cockburnianus* will reach 3 x 3m (10 x 10ft) after five years; the ground-covering *R. tricolor* will quickly reach a height of 60cm (24in) and spread to about 3-4m (10-13ft) after 12 years.
Pruning: Varies with species. Those, like *R.* 'Benenden', grown principally for their flowers, should have the oldest one-third of the shoots cut back to soil level each spring. Those, like *R. cockburnianus*, grown for their white winter stems, should be

completely cut back to soil level in early spring. Ground-cover varieties, such as *R. tricolor*, require no pruning but may be rejuvenated by cutting back to soil level in early spring (page 22).

Ruscus Butcher's broom

Size if unpruned: *Ruscus aculeatus* will attain 50 x 60cm (20 x 24in) after five years, and 1 x 1.2m (3 x 4ft) after 20 years.
Pruning: None essential but shoots are often damaged in winter and should be cut back to healthy growth or to soil level in spring (page 22).

Ruta Rue

Size if unpruned: *Ruta graveolens* and its popular variety 'Jackman's Blue' will reach its maximum size of about 75 x 60cm (30 x 24in) after two to three years.
Pruning: None essential, but two or three shoots may be removed at ground level each spring to encourage new growth (page 23), and the plants may be trimmed in early summer.

Rubus tricolor **can be rejuvenated by pruning back to soil level in spring**

51

Salix Willow

Size if unpruned: Many weeping willows, including *Salix x sepulcralis chrysocoma*, will reach 5 x 5m (16 x 16ft) after five years, 20 x 20m (65 x 65ft) after 20 years, and continue growing to 25 x 25m (80 x 80ft) after 40 years; however *S. caprea* 'Kilmarnock' and *S. purpurea* 'Pendula' will reach only about 3 x 3m (10 x 10ft) eventually and are often sold grafted as small weeping 'trees' which are smaller still; *S. alba* and *S. acutifolia* will reach about 6-7 x 1.5-2m (20-23 x 5-6½ft) after five years and 8-9 x 4.5-5.5m (25-30 x 14-17ft) after 20 years.
Pruning: None essential. However, those forms grown primarily for their attractive stems will benefit from being cut back hard each year or every other year in mid- to late spring (page 22); and weeping forms benefit from hard pruning back to just above the base or the graft junction every third spring.

Sambucus Elder

Size if unpruned: The beautiful cut-leaved golden elder, *Sambucus racemosa* 'Plumosa Aurea' will reach about 6 x 4m (20 x 13ft) after 20 years, *S. nigra* and its varieties half as tall again.
Pruning: There are two ways to

Solanum crispum looks best when allowed free rein but bear in mind that it can then easily swamp a small building

approach this: one option is to cut back the oldest one-third of the shoots to soil level each spring (page 23) to produce plants of the maximum size but generally with rather smaller leaves. Alternatively, cut the entire plant back to soil level in spring (page 22) to produce the best foliage but a smaller shrub overall and with little flower and fruit appeal.

Santolina Cotton lavender

Size if unpruned: *Santolina chamaecyparissus* will reach its maximum size of about 50 x 75cm (20 x 30in) after four or five years.
Pruning: Trim with shears in late spring, cutting just above the base of last year's growth.

Sarcococca Sweet box

Size if unpruned: *Sarcococca hookeriana* and its varieties will attain about 25 x 25cm (10 x 10in) after three years, 2 x 1m (6½ x 3ft) ultimately.
Pruning: None essential, but cut out any frost-damaged shoots in mid-spring.

Skimmia

Size if unpruned: Most forms, including the popular *Skimmia japonica* 'Rubella', will attain 40 x 40cm (16 x 16in) after five years, and 1 x 1m (3 x 3ft) after 20 years.
Pruning: None essential, and generally to be discouraged but cut out any winter-damaged shoots in mid-spring.

Solanum Potato vine, Potato tree

Size if unpruned: *Solanum crispum* 'Glasnevin' and similar varieties will attain 1.2 x 1.2m (4 x 4ft) after five years, and 3.8 x 3.8m (12 x 12ft) after 20 years.
Pruning: Climbing solanums look best

when allowed free rein, with over-crowded or damaged shoots being cut back to healthy wood in mid-spring.

Sorbus Mountain ash

Size if unpruned: Among the most popular of the tree-sized species, *Sorbus cashmiriana* will reach 2 x 2m (6½ x 6½ft) after five years and 4 x 4m (13 x 13ft) after 20 years; *S. hupehensis* and *S.* 'Joseph Rock' will reach 2.5 x 1.5m (8 x 5ft) after five years and 10 x 5m (33 x 16ft) after 20 years; *S. vilmorinii* will reach half this size.
Pruning: None, apart from removal of damaged branches in spring.

Spiraea

Size if unpruned: Most varieties will reach 1 x 1m (3 x 3ft) after five years, 2-2.5 x 2-2.5m (6½-8 x 6½-8ft) ultimately.
Pruning: *Spiraea* x *arguta* and *S. nipponica* (Bridal Wreath and Snowmound spiraeas) which flower early on the previous

Early flowering spiraeas require annual pruning, unlike the later flowering varieties

season's growth should have the oldest one-third of the dead flowered shoots cut back to soil level after flowering; *S. japonica* varieties, like 'Anthony Waterer', which flower later on the current year's shoots, may be left unpruned or cut back hard to soil level in early spring each year to stimulate new growth.

Stephanandra

Size if unpruned: *Stephanandra incisa* 'Crispa' will reach about 50 x 75cm (20 x 30in) after five years and about 1-1.5 x 1-1.5m (3-5 x 3-5ft) eventually; *S. tanakae* will reach about 1.5 x 1m (5 x 3ft) after five years and twice that eventually.
Pruning: None essential for *S. incisa* 'Crispa', but congested plants can be rejuvenated by cutting back some or all of the shoots to just above soil level in spring. *S. tanakae* should have the oldest third of the shoots cut back to soil level each spring, in order to produce new brown winter shoots (page 23).

Symphoricarpos Snowberry

Size if unpruned: *Symphoricarpos albus laevigatus* is a rather invasive plant that may reach 2.5 x 4-5m (8 x 13-16ft) after 15 years; varieties of *S. x doorenbosii* with attractively coloured fruits will reach only half this size.
Pruning: None essential if grown informally, but up to one-third of the oldest stems may be cut back to ground level in spring to produce new growth (page 23). For hedges see page 65.

Syringa Lilac

Size if unpruned: The common lilac *Syringa vulgaris* and the many variously coloured varieties usually grafted onto it will attain 2 x 2m (6½ x 6½ft) after five years, 6 x 6m (20 x 20ft) after 20 years;

Lilac varieties are usually grafted onto common lilac rootstock which will sucker freely

the dwarf species *S. meyeri* 'Palibin' will reach 30 x 25cm (12 x 10in) after five years, 1.5 x 1.2m (5 x 4ft) after 20 years.
Pruning: *S. vulgaris* should have all suckers removed in spring and autumn. Dead flowerheads should if possible be removed after flowering, to improve the appearance of the plant; and it will benefit from having up to one-third of the oldest or weakest shoots cut back to soil level in spring each year (page 23) although this is not essential. *S. meyeri* 'Palibin' requires no pruning.

Tamarix Tamarisk

Size if unpruned: Will attain about 1.5 x 1.5m (5 x 5ft) after five years, 3.5 x 3.5m (11 x 11ft) after 10 years.
Pruning: None is essential, but to prevent plants becoming leggy, early-flowering types such as *Tamarix tetrandra* should be pruned after flowering by cutting back the oldest one third of the shoots by at least half (page 21); and late-flowering types like *T. ramosissima* 'Rubra' should have all the old flowering shoots cut back by at least half in spring.

Taxus Yew

Size if unpruned: As a free-standing tree, the true species *Taxus baccata* may reach 15 x 10m (50 x 33ft) eventually although the popular selected forms such as 'Fastigiata' and 'Fastigiata Aureomarginata' will be much less than this.

Pruning: None essential although free-standing trees may develop misplaced branches and also clusters of sprouts or suckers on the trunk. These may be removed at any time of year. See also hedges and topiary page 64 and page 66.

Thuja Red cedar

Size if unpruned: The normal species *Thuja occidentalis* may attain 20 x 5m (65 x 16ft). Among its popular lower growing varieties, 'Rheingold' will reach 3-4 x 2-4m (10-13 x 6½-13ft); the very beautiful *T. orientalis* 'Aurea Nana' will only reach about 60 x 60cm (24 x 24in).

Pruning: None should be necessary but

Trachelospermum jasminoides is even more attractive when carefully tied to a wall

dwarf forms may be clipped in late spring. See also hedges page 64.

Thymus Thyme

Size if unpruned: Varies widely with variety. Within a four year span, the more vigorous bush forms such as 'Silver Posie' will reach 25 x 20cm (10 x 8in); the creeping forms such as 'Doone Valley', about 5 x 25cm (2 x 10in).

Pruning: Trim back dead flowerheads with shears after flowering (page 20), but remember that thymes are best treated as short-lived plants and after three or four years, no matter how carefully pruned, most tend to become straggly.

Trachelospermum Star jasmine

Size if unpruned: The two commonest and hardiest species, *Trachelospermum jasminoides* and *T. asiaticum* will attain about 1-1.5 x 1-1.5m (3-5 x 3-5ft) after five years, 4-5 x 4-5m (13-16 x 13-16ft) after 20 years.

Pruning: In spring remove any frost-damaged shoots, and cut back straggly side-shoots to within about 15cm (6in) of a permanent framework of stems to encourage flowering.

Tsuga Hemlock

Size if unpruned: *Tsuga canadensis* 'Pendula' can make a mound 3-5 x 3-5m (10-16 x 10-16ft), or a carpet about 50cm x 5m (20in x 16ft). In good conditions, *T. heterophylla* may reach 30 x 10m (100 x 33ft).

Pruning: None necessary. See also hedges page 64.

Ulex Gorse

Size if unpruned: Will reach about 75cm x 1m (30in x 3ft) after five

years and about 2 x 3m (6½ x 10ft) after 15 years.

Pruning: None necessary but old and neglected plants may be rejuvenated by cutting them back to soil level after flowering (page 19).

Vaccinium

Size if unpruned: Among predominantly flowering and foliage forms, *Vaccinium glaucoalbum* will reach about 75cm x 1m (30in x 3ft) eventually; *V. vitis-idaea* will reach a height of only 25cm (10in) but will spread as far as it is allowed to by underground runners.

Pruning: None necessary. For blueberries and other forms see page 74.

Viburnum

Size if unpruned: Among popular evergreen forms grown mainly for their winter and spring flowers, *Viburnum x burkwoodii* will reach 1.3 x 1.3m (4½ x 4½ft) after five years and 2.7 x 2.7m (9 x 9ft) after 20 years; *V. davidii* will reach 80 x 80cm (32 x 32in) after five years and 1.5 x 2m (5 x 6½ft) after 20 years; *V. rhytidophyllum* is very vigorous and will reach 1.5 x 1.5m (5 x 5ft) after five years and 5 x 5m (16 x 16ft) after 20 years. Among deciduous species, including *V. x bodnantense* and the varieties of *V. plicatum*, most will reach about 1.5 x 1m (5 x 3ft) after five years and about 3-5 x 3-4m (10-16 x 10-13ft) after 15 years but *V. carlesii* varieties are slower-growing and will reach only about 1.5-2 x 1.5-2m (5-6½ x 5-6½ft) in the same time.

Pruning: None necessary. For *V. tinus* grown as a hedge see page 64.

Vinca Periwinkle

Size if unpruned: *Vinca major* varieties will reach their maximum size of about 40cm x 1m (16in x 3ft) in five years;

ABOVE: The oldest third of the shoots on this *Viburnum bodnantense* should be cut out to encourage new growth and better flowering

V. minor varieties will reach a maximum of only about 15 x 80cm (6 x 32in) in the same time.

Pruning: None essential, but in order to rejuvenate plants they may be cut back every two or three years, in early spring. *V. major* can be cut to soil level with shears or a strimmer; *V. minor* should be trimmed more lightly.

Vitis Vine

Size if unpruned: Most ornamental vines reach about 3 x 3m (10 x 10ft) after

Strimming is the easiest way to cut back a large area of *Vinca major* and so encourage new shoots

five years; *V. coignetiae* will then reach about 12 x 12m (40 x 40ft) after 20 years; *V. vinifera* 'Brant' will reach about 9 x 9m (30 x 30ft); *V. vinifera* 'Purpurea' reaches about 6 x 6m (20 x 20ft).

Pruning: Ornamental vines may either be left unpruned to form an unruly but not unattractive tangle, if space permits, or they may be pruned like fruiting vines (page 90).

Weigela

Size if unpruned: Most popular varieties, including *Weigela florida* 'Foliis Purpureis' and 'Florida Variegata' will attain about 1.2 x 1.2m (4 x 4ft) after five years, and 2.3 x 2.3m (7½ x 7½ft) after 20 years.

Pruning: None essential, but mature plants will benefit from having the oldest one-third of the shoots cut back to the base each year after flowering (page 23).

Wisteria

Size if unpruned: *Wisteria floribunda* and its varieties will reach about 3 x 3m (10 x 10ft) after five years and 9 x 9m (30 x 30ft) after 20 years; *W. sinensis* and its forms will reach about 5 x 5m (16 x 16ft) after five years and 15 x 15m (50 x 50ft) or more after 20 years.

Pruning: In the first season after planting, loosely tie in all shoots to stout support wires. In the following winter, select three to five shoots to form the main framework of the plant, depending on the space available, cut them back by half, spread them out, spaced evenly, and tie them to the wires. After this, in late summer each year, cut back all long whippy side-shoots to about 25cm (10in), except for any required to fill in gaps in the main framework. In the following winter each year, cut these shortened shoots back further to three buds from their bases.

ROSES

" I have met gardeners who have been put off rose growing for no better reason than that they think that a large part of their year will be taken up with pruning. This is a seriously extreme view but there's no doubt that roses and pruning are inextricably linked in most people's minds. Let me reassure you. Yes, pruning is necessary with most types of rose; but no, it isn't difficult or very time-consuming. The situation has, unfortunately, been compounded by the fact that even very experienced and knowledgeable rose growers disagree on the best methods to follow and individual experts tend to have their own little eccentricities. And I know that many gardeners will have read or heard the suggestion that no pruning, in the accepted sense, is needed; that you can sweep across your plants with powered hedge trimmers and achieve as much success. I find this utter nonsense and so what you will find here is more conventional wisdom based on my own long experience of growing representatives of almost every main type of rose. "

General observations

Rose pruning isn't complicated but the different groups of roses do require rather different pruning techniques if the plants are to give of their best. I have outlined my preferred methods under eight main headings but, in every case, these operations follow the well established principles of pruning that I outlined earlier. I would also add the following general guidelines: in so far as it is possible, cut back Shrub and Bush

Roses (including Standards) to just above a bud that faces outwards, and Climbing and Rambling Roses to just above a bud that points upwards or in which ever other direction growth is needed to fill a gap.

Timing

There has been and probably always will be much argument about the timing of rose pruning; should it be done in autumn or spring? Generally, I don't prune in

Dead-heading should be performed regularly on all roses except those which will produce attractive autumn hips

56

Cankers and shoot die-backs should be cut out promptly, pruning well into the healthy wood

PRUNING METHOD 1

To be used with the following rose groups : Species Roses, most of the groups of Shrub Roses including Albas, Bourbons, Centifolias, some varieties of China Roses, Damasks, Gallicas, Hybrid Musks, Moss Roses, Noisettes, Rugosas, Hybrid Perpetuals, Polyanthas, Modern Shrubs, Tea Roses and Ground Cover Roses

Very little pruning is needed. Each year, cut out any damaged, dying or diseased shoots to a few centimetres above soil level and every two or three years, cut out one or two of the largest, thickest and oldest shoots in order to encourage regular shoot renewal. Sometimes, it's suggested that some of the main shoots should be shortened each year but I strongly discourage this as it produces a proliferation of shoots from the point of the cut, giving a mop-head appearance. Deadhead the flowers if the plants are small enough to enable this to be done but don't deadhead those varieties that produce attractive autumn hips.

Hard pruning of Hybrid Tea roses in the spring will help lessen the incidence of black spot

autumn. I find that in relatively cold areas, leaving on the old growth during the winter provides the plants with protection against hard frosts, which will, in any event, kill off some shoot growth. In mild areas, by contrast, autumn pruning can encourage the development of soft new growth during the winter; and this growth is then liable to be damaged by frost and cold winds in spring. So the only autumn pruning that I do is to remove abnormally long and whippy shoots on climbers or bush roses that would otherwise be blown around by winter winds and so physically moved and weakened in the soil. The only summer pruning, apart from deadheading, that I advocate is on Ramblers (see Methods 5 and 6).

PRUNING METHOD 2

To be used with the following rose groups: Floribundas and the larger Patio Roses

Each year, cut out any dead, damaged, feeble or dying shoots to a few centimetres above soil level. Then cut back, also to just above soil level, the oldest one-third of the shoots and finally, cut back the remaining shoots by one-third of their length.

PRUNING METHOD 3

To be used with the following rose groups: Hybrid Teas

Each year, cut out any dead, damaged, feeble or dying shoots to a few centimetres above soil level. Then cut back all remaining shoots by approximately half of their length.

PRUNING METHOD 4

To be used with the following rose groups: Miniature Roses and the smaller Patio Roses

The whole operation is best described as tidying up and should always be done in the spring, after the last hard frost. Cut back all dead and dying shoots (there will generally be a number of these) to just above soil level. Also thin out the number of shoots overall to eliminate congestion. Then cut back any long, old flowered shoots to approximately 10cm (4in) above the base of the plant, (many Miniatures produce flowering shoots at least double the height of the rest) and finally, cut back all remaining shoots by approximately one-third of their length.

Hybrid Tea rose 'Blue Moon' in spring before and after pruning. All of the shoots have been cut back by at least half (Pruning Method 3)

PRUNING METHOD 5

To be used with the following rose groups: Wichuraiana Ramblers (the rambling rose varieties like 'Dorothy Perkins' that are derived from *Rosa wichuraiana*)

When young, train the plants to form a framework. Then, each year, cut back up to one third of the old stems to just above soil level after flowering and cut back the old flowered side-shoots on the remainder to within about 10cm (4in) of their junction with the main stems.

PRUNING METHOD 6

To be used with the following rose groups: Multiflora Ramblers (the rambling rose varieties like 'Paul's Scarlet Climber' that are derived from *Rosa multiflora*). When young, train the plants to form a framework, then for the next two or three years, cut back the old flowered side-shoots after flowering to within about 10cm (4in) of their junction with the main stems. On older, established plants, cut back all old flowered stems to soil level after flowering.

PRUNING METHOD 7

To be used with the following rose groups: Species Climbers, Modern Climbers, Hybrid Musk Climbers, Bourbon Climbers

Very little pruning is needed. When young, train the plants to form a framework. Then, each year, cut out any dead, dying, diseased or crossing shoots, tie in any vigorous new shoots, bending them as close as possible to the

Floribunda rose 'Beautiful Britain' before and after spring pruning. One third of the shoots have been cut back to soil level and the remainder cut back by at least one third; in this instance rather harder than usual as they were growing weakly (Pruning Method 2)

Shrub rose 'Buff Beauty' before and after spring pruning. One large old shoot and a few weak shoots have been cut out; this may only need doing every two or three years (Pruning Method 1)

horizontal and cut out one or two old shoots each year if sufficient new shoots are available to replace them as part of the main framework. If there are insufficient new shoots, leave the main framework unpruned. After tying in, cut back any very long shoots to the available space.

PRUNING METHOD 8

To be used with the following rose groups: Noisette Climbers, Hybrid Perpetual Climbers, Climbing Tea Roses, Climbing Hybrid Teas, Climbing Floribundas

When young, train the plants to form a framework. Then, each year, cut back the old flowered side-shoots to within 10-15cm (4-6in) of their junction with the main framework. Every few years, replace one or two old shoots in the framework if sufficient vigorous new shoots are available to do this. If not, leave the main framework untouched.

Pruning standard roses

Standard Roses are shrub or bush varieties grafted on to rootstocks with a strong vertical stem. They should be pruned in the same way as their normal shrub or bush counterparts except that all pruning cuts are made relative, not to soil level or the base of the plant, but to the head, the position where the flowering variety has been budded.

Deadheading

As I've described earlier (on page 19), deadheading is the cutting away of the old flowered heads, partly in the cause of tidiness, but also to lessen the likelihood of diseases becoming established. It also encourages new buds to burst and, with repeat or continuous-flowering roses, so result in a fresh crop of flowers later in

Miniature roses almost invariably produce a mass of congested stems and will need thinning out each spring (Pruning Method 4)

the season. The only rose varieties that shouldn't be deadheaded are the Species and Shrub Roses that produce attractive hips in the autumn; and also, of course, those plants that are simply too big to manage.

As with everything else in rose growing, there are differing opinions on how far the old flowered shoots should be cut back but I adhere to the more traditional approach that has served me well: I cut back to just above the first leaflet with five, rather than three leaflets, and a strong outward facing bud.

Pruning rose hedges

There is little point in growing roses as hedging plants if they are hard pruned or clipped in the way that more formal hedges are treated, for this will simply remove the flower buds. My advice therefore is to treat them as exactly what

A *Rosa gallica officinalis* hedge. Almost no pruning is needed if appropriate varieties have been chosen; *Rosa rugosa* is another popular choice

they are – a long line of flowering shrubs – and perform the minimum amount of pruning consistent with keeping them tidy. In many instances, almost no pruning will be required other than the removal of the occasional dead or feeble shoot.

HEDGES

❝ *Hedges are the strongest and most ornamental of garden boundaries and, depending on the local climate, there is an enormous variety of suitable plants from which you can choose. Some provide an excellent foil for other plants, some are dramatically colourful in their own right; some play a valuable role in deterring intruders or hiding neighbours, others attract beneficial (and of course, a few not so beneficial) insects or other wildlife, some can be exquisitely formal, others quaintly rustic. Every garden should have at least some hedging but the various types have differing advantages and disadvantages in respect of pruning. I suggest the number of times each year that different types should be trimmed, these are really minimum requirements. Rather like a lawn, a hedge will look better the more frequently it is cut. Always remember, however, that for the first cuts of the year, birds may be nesting and you must check that none will be disturbed by your activities.* ❞

Formal hedges

The two main factors to consider when choosing hedging plants are speed of growth, and whether the plants should be deciduous or evergreen. The best formal hedging plants, box and yew, both have a reputation for slow growth. Box is, indeed, fairly slow but the reputation with yew is quite unjustified; after the first season, it will put on 30cm (12in) of main shoot elongation per year although, of course, some of this must be cut back (see below). Once established, both box

and yew should ideally be cut twice a year although once will suffice. By contrast, fast-growing conifers, especially the cypresses, must be cut several times each summer. Although evergreen hedges will provide an all-year-round barrier, they sometimes present pruning problems. Laurel, for example, is very hard to trim neatly unless you do it carefully by hand because the large leaves look unattractive when sliced through with shears. And many conifers undeniably make dull

hedges. Beech and, to a lesser extent, hornbeam, which although deciduous, retain their leaves late into the winter, make attractive compromises.

The aim in pruning a formal hedge is to maintain an even shape and a dense surface. It is advisable to make the hedge

A newly planted hedge of hawthorn with the plants being cut back to about 15cm (6in) to encourage bushy growth

wider at the bottom than at the top, sloping the sides at an angle of 15-25 degrees (this is known as a 'batter'), in order to allow equal amounts of light to reach all parts. Lack of light and inadequate initial pruning are the main causes of gaps at the base of a hedge.

Plants suitable for formal hedges may be divided into three groups requiring three different approaches to pruning:

GROUP I

This is made up of deciduous and evergreen species that require hard pruning initially to encourage dense growth. Without careful pruning the hedge will be thin at the base. Included are the deciduous *Crataegus* (hawthorn), *Prunus cerasifera* (myrobalan plum), *P. spinosa* (blackthorn), *Symphoricarpos* (snowberry), and *Tamarix* (tamarisk). Evergreens in this category include: *Buxus sempervirens* (box), *Escallonia, Ligustrum* (privet), and *Lonicera nitida*.

Formative pruning: The deciduous species should be planted between mid-autumn and early spring, and immediately cut back to 15cm (6in) from soil level. The evergreens should ideally be planted in early to mid-spring (although autumn is satisfactory in mild areas) and cut back by one-third. Privet, which is semi-evergreen, is best planted in spring but cut back to 15cm (6in). I then do no pruning in the first full year of growth.

In late winter or early spring in the second season after planting, the main shoots of the deciduous species should be cut back by about half. Any side-shoots should be cut back to within 5-8cm (2-3½in) of the main stems. This hard pruning may need to be repeated again a year later if the base of the hedge is still thin. A year after planting, evergreens should be pruned by about one-third.

Early in the summer of the third year

By cutting a hedge, such as this beech hedge, with a batter (narrower at the top), growth will be thicker; and in cold areas, damage from snow is less likely

after planting, begin trimming the hedge to form a batter. For the first few years this will need to be done several times during the summer to create a dense surface. The top of the hedge should be trimmed lightly in late summer until it reaches the required height.

Pruning the established hedge: Most species in this group, including *Lonicera nitida* and privet, will need to be trimmed three or four times each summer, between late spring and early autumn. Others that are slower growing, including

Fast growing hedges like privet must be pruned several times each year as they soon become untidy

box, will need trimming only once, in mid- to late summer.

GROUP 2

This includes deciduous species that are naturally bushy at the base, such as *Carpinus betulus* (hornbeam), *Corylus* (hazel), *Fagus sylvatica* (beech), *Forsythia* and *Ribes* (flowering currant). The initial pruning with these species is less drastic than with plants in Group 1.

Formative pruning: After planting, which should be between mid-autumn and early spring, cut back the main stem and all strong side-shoots by one-third. Repeat this a year later to ensure strong, bushy growth. The top should be only lightly tidied until the hedge reaches the required height.

Pruning the established hedge: In the summer of the third year after planting, start trimming the hedge to a neat shape with a batter. This should preferably be in early summer and again in late summer or early autumn or, alternatively, just once in late summer. Beech and hornbeam will normally need trimming only once, in late summer. Flowering hedges, such as forsythia, should be trimmed immediately after flowering, and again lightly in late summer.

GROUP 3

This includes evergreen species such as x *Cupressocyparis leylandii* (Leyland cypress), *Ilex* (holly), *Pyracantha* and *Taxus baccata* (yew), together with those aromatic plants sometimes used for dwarf hedging, lavender, rosemary, thyme and santolina, which need only light pruning at first.

Formative pruning: After planting, in autumn or spring, leave leading shoots unpruned but trim any wayward side-shoots. In colder areas, the plants should be protected in some way against the drying effect of the wind for the first year

Carefully clipped, yew will give a neater appearance than other plants

or two, (at least during the winter), ideally with a temporary fence or with plastic mesh.

Starting in the second or third year after planting (depending on how well and how quickly it has become established), the leading shoot of each plant should be cut back by half in late summer and until it reaches the required height. Trimming the sides to produce a batter should also

start in the third summer, to encourage a dense surface. This should be done two or three times between late spring and early autumn.

Pruning the established hedge: Fast-growing species such as Leyland cypress should be cut twice, in early summer and again in late summer. The slower-growing species such as holly and yew will need to be cut only once, in late summer. Flowering species, such as pyracanthas, should have new growth cut back in the second half of the summer to avoid losing too many flowers and fruits.

Informal hedges

Many flowering and berrying shrubs make attractive informal hedges, for example *Berberis* x *stenophylla*, the smaller *B. thunbergii* varieties, *Cotoneaster simonsii*, *Deutzia*, *Fuchsia* and rugosa roses. The aim in pruning these hedges is to allow blossom and fruits to form a looser, more natural surface, rather than cutting back and losing them.

The plants should be pruned in the same way as when they are grown as free-standing shrubs (see relevant pages), mainly by cutting back old wood. Those that flower on the current season's wood, such as hardy fuchsias, should be pruned in spring, and those that flower on old wood, such as *Berberis* x *stenophylla*, should be pruned immediately after flowering. Shrubs that produce ornamental berries, such as *Cotoneaster*, should be pruned after the berries have disappeared.

Aromatic plants such as lavender, rosemary, thyme and santolina, although best when clipped formally (see above), may also be used to form fragrant informal low hedges. They should then be pruned in the same way as when they are free-standing.

Renovating a hedge

If you inherit a badly neglected hedge, it may be possible to restore it by drastic pruning, in conjunction with feeding, watering and mulching. Yew responds particularly well to this treatment, holly, beech, hornbeam and privet moderately so, box less satisfactorily as it doesn't regenerate well from old wood. With the plants that don't regenerate as well, some moderate cutting back may need to be combined with planting new plants alongside or to fill in gaps. Do remember, however, that the soil here will be highly impoverished and must be generously improved with organic matter and fertilizer, with special attention given to watering after planting. Renovation pruning of deciduous hedges is best done during the dormant period, in late winter, and of evergreens in mid- to late-spring, but not when it is frosty.

Only one side of the hedge should be cut back at first. Cut the top down to the required height, and then cut all of the branches on one side back to the main stems. Only when the cut side is growing back strongly should the other side be pruned in the same way. This may be a year later, but is more likely take two years.

Some severely overgrown and tangled deciduous hedges may be very effectively and very beautifully restored by laying (not to be confused with layering). This technique involves the cutting away of much of the upper growth and inserting within the hedge itself a framework of vertical stakes and horizontal wooden members. The main stems of the hedge plant themselves are then cut through half way, bent over at an angle of 45 degrees and secured to the framework. Laying can only be done with species that have sufficiently pliable wood and will regenerate well from old shoots. Hawthorn is much the most responsive, but the task is a skilled one and best left to an expert. In rural areas, most farmers will know of someone skilled in hedge laying.

Informal, flowering hedges, like this *Ribes sanguineum* should be pruned in the same way as equivalent free-standing shrubs

TOPIARY

" *Topiary, once considered among the most elusive and challenging of its arts, has become both accessible and popular in recent years. It is simply enough defined as the clipping of ornamental trees and shrubs to fanciful shapes, and is an ancient craft (a Roman word for a gardener was* topiarius*). Examples can be found all over the world; among the finest are reckoned to be growing in an Ecuadorian cemetery. One reason that topiary has become more widely available is that ready-clipped shrubs may be purchased in containers, but they are costly items. The parallel increased availability of metal topiary frames means that there is now no excuse for gardeners not to try it for themselves. I have done much topiary, both* de novo *and by adapting existing shrubs, and experience has brought home to me one important fact that I gladly share: unless you positively enjoy being frustrated by your workmanship, don't try to create two (or more) perfectly matching topiary items. You will be driven mad in the attempt.* "

Choice of plant

Topiary is merely an application of the techniques of hedge-pruning and interesting shapes can be achieved within a few years. Although all manner of shrubs have been clipped to topiary shapes at one time or another,

Yew is undoubtedly the best topiary plant but even then, perfect symmetry is very difficult to achieve

conventional (and simple) topiary requires evergreen shrubs with small leaves, fairly flexible stems, a dense, much branched habit, a good response to clipping and, of course, hardiness. The best by far is yew, followed by box, which is especially good for small specimens up to about 2m (6½ft) high, while for larger, simpler shapes, holly, Portugal laurel, bay laurel and holm oak are suitable, as are some of the cypresses, although these are really too fast growing to be other than a chore. I have seen laurel used for topiary but its leaves really are too big (though it might make a good armadillo). Coloured or variegated leaf forms of all of these plants can be blended with all-green varieties to create dramatic and very effective forms. Although considered cheating by purists, small-leaved ivies can very effectively be trained over a pre-formed shape and will soon take on the appearance of a 'real' shrub. Deciduous plants are rarely used, although hawthorn can satisfactorily be trimmed to a neat shape. Privet isn't ideal, as it gives a coarse surface, needs frequent trimming, and can be bare in a cold winter.

Choosing a shape

The shape chosen should ideally be bold and simple, if it's to be fairly easily maintained.

Rounded shapes are much easier to create and are more manageable than geometrically angular or fanciful ones. Spheres and cones can reasonably easily be trained without a frame and then cut free-hand. Pyramids are among the more popular geometrical forms and these are relatively easy with a frame. Animal shapes (birds especially) are popular but you will be a skilled topiarist indeed if you can manage to make these without a frame.

LEFT: **Box is one of the best choices for topiary after yew but is seldom of such dense habit**

BELOW: **Holly has the advantage of offering variegated foliage to topiary subjects**

TOPIARY

Establishing your specimen: Frames for training topiary may be placed in the open ground or in containers. Complex ones are best bought but simple, regular shapes can be made with canes or with canes and wire. Choose plants with plenty of branches and no obvious dead shoots or areas of die-back. For large topiary subjects, more than one plant may be used, either deliberately allowing each stem to be visible for special effect (the legs of an animal for instance) or by encouraging leafy growth from the base to conceal the fact. Tie in all shoots within reach of the frame and clip back any parts

Fanciful shapes such as these birds are formed over a metal frame

that 'stray' outside. I use oiled garden twine for tying. It's flexible and easy to use and durable enough to last for three or four years, yet it will eventually decay and won't, as wire does, strangle the stems in time. It is very important to continue tying in the stems while they are young and flexible. Shoots that are entirely within the frame should be trimmed lightly to encourage them to branch.

How to clip: Large specimens can be trimmed with hand shears or with electric hedge-trimmers. More detailed work should be done with single-handed shears. Larger-leaved plants, such as bay laurel, should be pruned with secateurs,

removing whole leaves or clusters of leaves at a time. In general, trim lightly at first, checking the shape constantly; remember, it's always possible to cut more from the plant, but you can never put it back.

Frequency of clipping: All topiary subjects should be cut fairly frequently. Slower-growing plants, such as box and yew, should be cut at least twice, in midsummer and early autumn; fast-growing ones such as privet will need to be trimmed three or four times between late spring and early autumn. It makes sense never to prune during very cold weather, however, as cold winds or frost can bring about die-back through the cut surfaces.

Tie young shoots to the frame to give uniform coverage

Making use of existing shrubs: It isn't necessary to start with new plants. Topiary is one way of reducing the size of an overgrown bush, or turning an unwanted plant into an attractive feature, something that I have done in my own garden with an ancient but misshapen box. Other than with yew, this kind of operation must, however, be spread over two or three seasons, for while you can cut back yew very hard into old wood, with every expectation that it will sprout anew, other shrubs just aren't as co-operative and you should cut back into wood no older than three years initially. If this sprouts, you might try wood slightly older but my advice is to make the best shape you can without cutting into wood more than three years old.

Renovating topiary: If a specimen has been neglected, damaged or diseased, it may be possible, especially with yew, box or holly to restore the shape by cutting back excess growth and cutting into old wood. It may be wise to spread this work over several years, rather than doing it all at once; and it must be combined with balanced feeding and watering.

If a hole has developed this may not be so easy to repair, as the pruning necessary to generate new growth will make the hole even bigger for a long time.

One solution is to alter the shape of the specimen, using both pruning and training, although even this may take several years to complete. Another option, as with repairing hedges, is to place additional new plants alongside.

Clip away extraneous shoots and the pattern will begin to develop

SOFT FRUIT

" *Attention to pruning is probably more important with soft fruit than with any other edible crop. And with the exception of modern roses and some climbers, it's probably more important than with any other type of garden plant. There are few sights in the garden more pathetic than that of unpruned soft fruit; yet there are few sights aesthetically more pleasing than a group of canes or bushes, neatly and correctly pruned and trained. In all instances, the pruning is both logical and straightforward but it does differ markedly between the different types of soft fruit and, in some instances, even between different varieties or forms of the same crop; so pay attention.* "

Raspberry

Modern raspberries are divided into two groups: those that fruit on the canes produced in the previous season (the majority) and those primocane varieties like 'Autumn Bliss' that fruit in the autumn on the tips of the current season's canes.

TRAINING

When planting, preferably in late autumn, cut back the canes to just above a bud about 25cm (10in) above soil level. I find it better if the plants aren't allowed to fruit in their first summer (in order to prevent this, any flowers should be removed as soon as they appear) although this isn't critical, especially in good soil. As the plant grows, tie in all of the strong canes to horizontal training wires, and cut out weak ones or any that have grown too far away from the wires. The top training wire should be about 1.2m (4ft) high

It's impossible to grow raspberries successfully without properly spaced horizontal support wires

(see *Best Soft Fruit* for details of establishing a system of training wires). In late winter of each year, cut off the top of each cane to no more than 25cm (10in) taller than the top wire and train the tip horizontally along it.

Pruning Summer-fruiting varieties: After the fruit has been picked, the canes that have borne fruit are of no more use and should be cut off at soil level. The new green canes that have, in the meantime, appeared should be tied in

Autumn fruiting raspberries should be pruned completely down to soil level in early spring

Pruning: After planting, preferably in late autumn, cut back the canes to just above a bud about 25cm (10in) above soil level. As new canes appear during the following spring, they should be tied in to horizontal wires. Much the simplest method is called the single-bay system, which utilises a fan pattern of training (see *Best Soft Fruit* for alternative methods). If the canes outgrow their allotted space, the tips should be removed. As new canes emerge during the season, these should be tied vertically to the support wires, the older, fruiting canes being moved outwards, in a fan pattern, to be re-tied outside the new ones.

In early autumn each year, just after the fruit has been picked, the fruit-bearing canes should be cut off at soil level and the new canes should be re-tied in their place. About 24 canes per parent plant

their place. Any that have grown more than about 25cm (10in) from the wires should be removed, preferably by being pulled up to discourage re-growth; and any excess canes should be cut out, leaving about eight or nine canes per metre (yard) of wire, or about five or six canes to each parent plant.

Pruning Autumn-fruiting varieties: Autumn-fruiting or primocane varieties should be pruned during the second half of the winter by cutting all canes back to soil level. The new fruit-bearing canes will grow up within a few weeks.

Blackberry

Several new varieties of blackberry have recently been developed with the intention of rivalling the taste of the wild blackberry, but making a more manageable plant. All varieties are pruned in the same way.

should be allowed to grow and fruit each year; any extra or weak ones should be cut out. Any suckers that appear too far away from the plant should be pulled out if possible, or cut away with a spade.

Loganberry and other hybrid berries

The loganberry is the oldest raspberry-blackberry hybrid, but there are many others, including the Boysenberry, the Hildaberry, the King's Acre berry, the Phenomenal berry, the Silvanberry, the Sunberry, the Tayberry, the Tummelberry, the Veitchberry, and the Youngberry. The Wineberry is a true species, *Rubus phoenicolasius*, the Marionberry also possibly a species but could be another raspberry-blackberry cross. All are grown and pruned exactly as blackberries.

Remove the old fruited canes from blackberries and related hybrid fruits like this loganberry immediately after the fruit have been picked

Blackcurrant

❝ Unlike red currants, white currants and gooseberries, blackcurrants aren't amenable to cordon or other restricted training methods and must be grown as free-standing bushes. Many new varieties have been raised in recent years with the frost hardiness and pest and disease resistance bred in. Unfortunately, most are very large plants. Only one variety, 'Ben Sarek', has been bred with gardeners in mind. It is a small, compact, high yielding mid-season variety which should always be the first choice for home garden use. ❞

Pruning: After planting, ideally in early winter, all shoots should be cut back to just above two buds from the base.

At the end of the first fruiting season, when the number of branches on the new plant should have at least doubled, cut back one or two to just above two buds from the base, and also cut out any weak shoots, cutting back to their junction with the parent branch.

The best fruit is produced on one-year-old wood; two- and three-year-old wood will produce good crops, but anything older will produce very little. The subsequent pruning, therefore, is directed accordingly. In the second year, and in each subsequent year, cut back the oldest one-quarter or one-third of the shoots to just above the base, as well as any that are hanging very close to the ground (where the fruit will become contaminated with soil). Also cut out any weak or damaged shoots. This may be done at any time between the ripening of the fruit and midwinter; some gardeners choose to do it when they are harvesting the crop.

Prune newly planted blackcurrants to just above soil level

Red currant and White currant

❝ I simply couldn't garden without red and white currants and I can't understand why every gardener doesn't feel the same about these utterly splendid plants. They are descended from three wild species of Ribes, and are more closely related to each other and to gooseberries than they are to blackcurrants. They produce large quantities of delicious and versatile fruits that can be eaten fresh or frozen. ❞

Pruning: as for gooseberry.

Red and white currants are most conveniently grown as cordons, against horizontal support wires

Gooseberry

An undeniable drawback to gooseberry growing is their thorns: no-one has yet succeeded in breeding a satisfactory, entirely thornless variety. This is where training and pruning come to the rescue as it's possible to make gooseberry picking less painful by growing them as cordons or other restricted forms. Although gooseberries are divided into dessert and culinary varieties, this is only determined by the relative acidity of the fruit, and pruning is identical for all varieties.

Pruning: gooseberries may be grown as free-standing bushes, as fans against a wall, or as cordons against horizontal wires. Each method entails different training but essentially similar pruning.

Bushes: the aim is to produce a goblet-shaped plant with an open centre that you can reach into without being scratched. In the first winter after planting, cut out any branches at the centre of the bush, and cut back the remaining branches by about one-third, to just above a bud. With naturally upright growing varieties, this should be an outward-facing bud, to avoid crowding; in spreading varieties, it should be inward-facing, to encourage the growth of more upright branches that will be better able to bear the weight of the fruit.

In the following winter, repeat the cutting back process; by now there should be eight to 10 branches, which is the maximum number required. About six weeks after midsummer in every subsequent year, cut back the leading shoots of each branch by about one-third, and any side-shoots on them to just

above six leaf-clusters from their base. Every winter, cut back the leading shoots of each branch again by one-third, and all side-shoots to two buds from their base. Also remove any branches that grow up

from the middle of the plant, and any suckers from below soil level. Occasionally you may need to train a new branch to replace one that is damaged.

Cordons: think of a cordon as one, two or three branches (single, double or triple cordons) trained vertically against a wall; and remember that the pruning is essentially similar to that of a branch growing normally on a bush. In winter, after planting, select the strongest vertical branch(es) to tie in to the support wires, and cut out the remainder. About six weeks after midsummer in the following year, cut back all side-shoots to just above the sixth leaf-cluster from their bases, but leave the leading shoot untouched. In winter, cut the side-shoots back again, to two buds from the base, and cut the leader back by about one-third. Continue this process until the leader reaches the top of the wires; from then on treat it in the same way as the side-shoots.

Fans: the branches of a fan are simply trained flat against a wall using training wires, each one being treated like a cordon and any side branches that emerge directly towards or away from the wall being cut off at the base.

Worcesterberry

This is a cross between a gooseberry and a blackcurrant. It bears fairly small, very dark red, fairly sweet fruit in fairly large quantities, on plants similar to gooseberries.

All cordon plants, such as gooseberries and red or white currants should be tied to vertical canes which are, in turn, tied to the horizontal support wires

ACID-SOIL FRUITS

Blueberry

❝ Vaccinium corymbosum, the highbush blueberry, will grow to a height of 3.5m (11ft) if allowed. It prefers a mild climate as well as acid soil, although some of the newer varieties are more cold tolerant. The best variety that I have seen is 'Blue Crop', with a good flavour, early to mid-season cropping, fairly high yield, and vigorous. Although the plants are self-fertile, the flowers open at different times, and so it makes sense to grow more than one variety to ensure pollination. ❞

Pruning: the same as for blackcurrants; the aim is to stimulate the regular growth of new shoots from the base of the plant.

Cranberry

❝ Although it belongs to the same genus as the blueberry, the cranberry looks quite different: it is a low-growing, wiry bush. Although there are wild European cranberries, the cultivated varieties are derived from the American Vaccinium macrocarpon which has larger, juicier fruits than the European species. Probably the two best types for gardeners are the unimaginatively named 'C. N.', with large red fruits, and a mat-forming habit, and 'Franklin', with smaller, darker fruits, and less vigorous growth. ❞

Pruning: none necessary except to cut away any damaged shoots in spring.

Unlike the wild European cranberry, American cranberries *Vaccinium macrocarpon*, are upright bushy plants in need of little or no pruning

LEFT: Blueberries are most effectively grown in containers and should be pruned like blackcurrants

" Many gardeners wonder why they need to go to the trouble of pruning fruit trees when nature manages perfectly well without, and the fact that old, established fruit trees need very little pruning compounds the mystery. But plant a young fruit tree and do nothing and you will soon discover the answer. Within a few years, the tree will become a tangle of crossing branches and its productivity will always be feeble, perhaps no worse than that of a wild tree, but immeasurably worse than a cultivated variety that has been carefully pruned and trained in its early years.

Numerous different training and pruning methods have been devised for fruit trees, especially apples and pears, over the years. I am limiting myself here to those relative few that are the most useful and easy for garden use. "

Rootstocks: Before considering pruning, I must say something about fruit tree rootstocks because the size and, to a degree, the shape of a modern fruit tree (especially an apple) depends at least as much on the rootstock on which it is grafted as on pruning method, fruiting variety or site factors. A modern fruit nursery will be able to supply (sometimes to special order), any variety grafted on to any rootstock so if you are buying new trees, do check that the rootstock will give you the size of tree you require. You will spend (literally) an almost fruitless lifetime trying to keep a tree that has been grafted on a vigorous rootstock to a small size simply by pruning.

The use of dwarfing and semi-dwarfing rootstocks means that even a mature apple tree remains a resonable size

Apples

Rootstocks: M 27: extremely dwarfing, suitable for container-grown or 'step-over' trees (page 77); plants may need staking throughout their lives and must be grown in very fertile soil; crop after two years. Height after 10 years: 1.5m (5ft).

M 9: dwarfing, suitable for small cordon or dwarf bush trees; may need staking throughout their lives and very fertile soil; crop after two to three years. Height after 10 years: 2m (6 1/2ft).

M 26: moderately dwarfing, suitable for small espaliers, cordons (especially for fruit tunnels), small fans or bush trees; will tolerate less good conditions; free-standing trees will need staking for six to seven years; crop after two to three years. Height after 10 years: 2.5m (8ft).

MM 106: semi-vigorous, suitable for general purpose garden trees, probably the most widely available rootstock; need staking for first three to four years; crop after three to four years. Height after 10 years: 3.5m (11ft).

MM 111: vigorous: suitable for traditional orchards, for large espaliers or large fans but too vigorous for cordons; may need staking for first two to three years; very tolerant of drought and poor soil, will grow readily through grass; crop after six to seven years. Height after 10 years: 5m (16ft).

Planting: Apple trees are normally bought as 'maidens' or 'maiden whips': one-year-old trees consisting of the growth made during the first season after the fruiting apple variety or 'scion wood' was budded or grafted on to the rootstock. Some maidens are 'feathered', that is, they have lateral shoots along their stems. Apples are best planted as bare-rooted trees during the dormant season, preferably in late autumn.

The principle of pruning for fruit production: Most apples bear their fruit on stubby shoots or 'spurs' that grow on older wood (page 7). Some spurs form naturally, but they can be encouraged to develop by spur pruning, a process that is generally carried out in late summer on restricted forms such as cordons and espaliers, and between late autumn and late winter on free-standing trees or bushes. Irrespective of the training method chosen, it's important to appreciate the principle. Spur pruning should begin between the second and fifth year after planting, depending largely on the rootstock and the training method adopted. The smaller the tree, as determined by the rootstock, the sooner it will start bearing fruit.

In the first year, cut back all one-year-old side-shoots, or 'maiden laterals', to four buds from their bases. The following year, the lateral will produce one or two shoots from its tip, and flower buds will develop close to its base. (Flower buds are plump and furry, while wood buds are smooth and pointed). Once these flower

TREE FRUIT

The rootstock M 26 is the most useful for creating a fruit tunnel, one of the most attractive features in any kitchen garden

> **❝** *The shape into which you should train your tree will depend on the space available. Cordons, espaliers, and fans are most appropriate where space is very limited, dwarf bushes and bush trees are most suited to small gardens. A bush tree will normally have a clear stem of about 50cm (20in) from soil level to the lowest branch. A half-standard tree has a trunk of about 1.2 m (4ft), and a standard tree has a trunk of about 2m (6½ft). Standards and half-standards will be slower to start bearing fruit, and ladders will be required to prune and harvest.* **❞**

CORDONS

Formative pruning: Cordons may be trained vertically or diagonally. Vertical cordons are sometimes called minarette trees. These shouldn't be confused with Ballerina, Columnar or Pole trees which require little pruning but are, I find, much less satisfactory. For diagonal cordons, the tree is planted at an angle of 45 degrees with the grafting union above ground and the scion (fruiting variety) wood uppermost. In order to form a cordon, immediately after planting a maiden tree, cut back all side-shoots more than 10cm (4in) long to three buds from their base. Don't prune the leading shoot, but tie it in to permanent supports. No further winter pruning will be required.

The tree should be discouraged from fruiting during the following year. If flowers appear in the spring, remove them carefully without damaging the leaves at their base. When the leading shoot reaches the required height, cut it back in late spring to about 15cm (6in) above the top wire. From then on, cut

buds have formed, cut back the shoot to just above the topmost flower bud.

Each flower bud will produce four or five blossoms, and each blossom at least one fruit. Behind this fruit, new flower buds will form, and a 'spur system' of flower buds on tiny gnarled branches will develop, and renew itself. After a few years the spur systems may become overcrowded. It is then necessary to thin them by cutting out any weaker spurs, or those on the undersides of the branches.

An alternative method of pruning for fruit is 'renewal pruning'. Here, maiden laterals are left unpruned in the first winter. By the second winter, flower buds will have formed on the older growth, and all of the recent season's growth is removed. Fruit will be borne all along the shoot in the following year, and after it has been harvested the shoot is cut back to about 2.5cm (1in) from its base. By the winter of the following year a strong new lateral will have grown out of this stub, and the process is then repeated.

Cordons, planted diagonally, offer the facility to grow a large number of varieties in a very small area. The twice a year pruning needed is all within easy reach

and tie them into support wires. If one is weak, cut it back by about one-third to an upward facing bud. Otherwise, do not prune. At the same time, in order to create the next tier, prune back the central stem to about 45cm (18in) above the lower branches, again just above three strong buds. Cut back any other shoots to three buds.

In the following summers, as before, tie in the side branches at first at an angle of 45 degrees, and then in late autumn lower them to the horizontal.

Continue this system of summer and autumn pruning until the required number of tiers has been formed, at which point the central leader stem should be cut back in summer to check further growth.

Pruning for fruit production: The arms of the espalier are maintained in a similar way to a cordon in order to encourage fruiting. In the summer of the second year after planting, any side-shoots more than 20cm (8in) long growing out from the arms should be cut back to three leaves above the base, and at the same time any small shoots growing out of the side-shoots should be cut back to one leaf. To prevent the central stem and the arms from growing too long, cut them back in late spring, removing nearly all of the previous summer's growth. If branches don't always arise where you require them in establishing your espalier, train the strongest shoot nearest your ideal position. If you find that there are still gaps in the framework, try the nicking and notching technique described on page 19.

back all but 2.5cm (1in) of its growth each summer.

Pruning for fruit production: In the second mid- or late summer after planting, cut back any side-shoots more than 20cm (8in) long growing directly from the main stem to a point just above the third leaf cluster from the base. At the same time, cut back any side-shoots growing out of spur systems to just one leaf above their bases. Repeat this process each year.

ESPALIERS

An espalier consists of a central stem bearing tiers of paired horizontal branches, trained flat against a wall or support wires. The branches are normally 40-45cm (16-18in) apart. A type of apple tree called a 'step-over' tree has become popular for edging paths and beds, especially in small gardens. These are simply espaliers with only one tier of branches very close to ground level.

Formative pruning: After planting an unfeathered maiden in winter, cut it back to 40cm (16in) above soil level, just above three plump buds. The top-most of these buds will grow to become the central stem, and the two below will develop as the two lowest branches (see page 78).

In mid- or late summer tie the top shoot in to a vertical cane, and the two lower ones to canes placed at angles of 45 degrees. If one of the side branches is growing weakly, raise it higher; if one is growing too vigorously, lower it.

Then, in late autumn, carefully lower the two branches so they are horizontal,

Of all the ways in which fruit trees may be trained, I find the espalier the most satisfying, practical and aesthetically pleasing. Unfortunately, many gardeners shy away from espaliers, believing them difficult to train and establish. I have chosen this form of tree for step by step illustrations therefore and hope that as a result of this reassurance, espaliers will sprout forth in gardens everywhere.

ESTABLISHED PLANTS

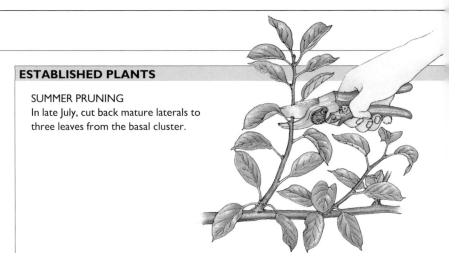

SUMMER PRUNING
In late July, cut back mature laterals to three leaves from the basal cluster.

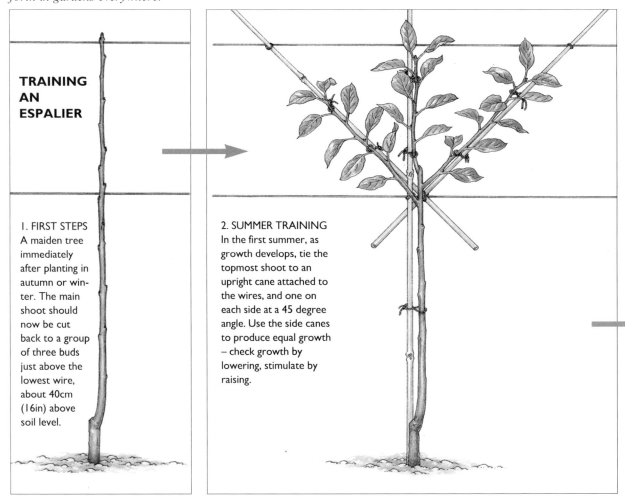

TRAINING AN ESPALIER

1. FIRST STEPS
A maiden tree immediately after planting in autumn or winter. The main shoot should now be cut back to a group of three buds just above the lowest wire, about 40cm (16in) above soil level.

2. SUMMER TRAINING
In the first summer, as growth develops, tie the topmost shoot to an upright cane attached to the wires, and one on each side at a 45 degree angle. Use the side canes to produce equal growth – check growth by lowering, stimulate by raising.

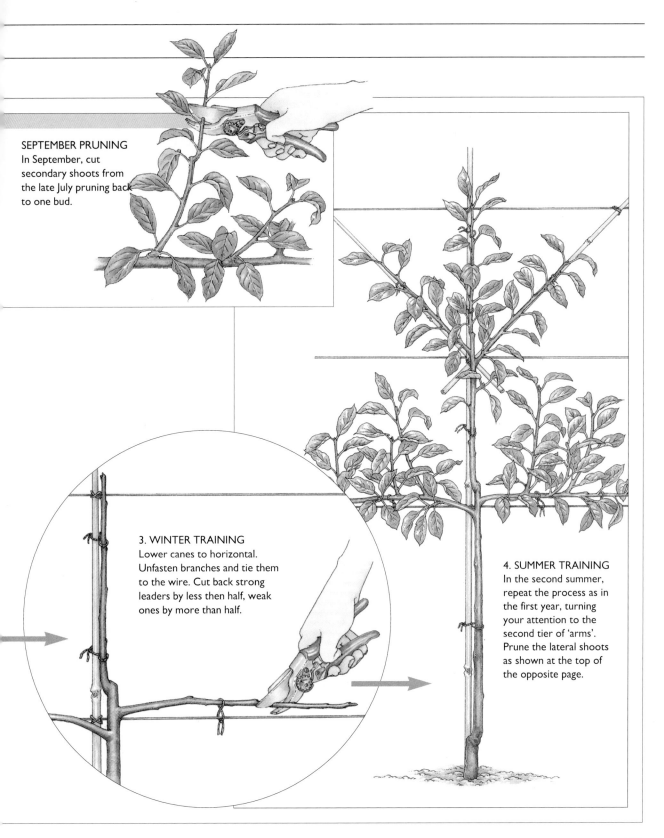

SEPTEMBER PRUNING
In September, cut secondary shoots from the late July pruning back to one bud.

3. WINTER TRAINING
Lower canes to horizontal. Unfasten branches and tie them to the wire. Cut back strong leaders by less then half, weak ones by more than half.

4. SUMMER TRAINING
In the second summer, repeat the process as in the first year, turning your attention to the second tier of 'arms'. Prune the lateral shoots as shown at the top of the opposite page.

OPEN-CENTRED BUSHES AND TREES

This is the most popular and successful shape for apple trees and bushes, as it exposes the fruit to maximum sunshine and air. The aim is to create a goblet shape, or an upside-down umbrella.

Formative pruning: After planting a maiden tree in winter, cut back the leading shoot by up to one-third, or to the required height, cutting above a plump bud. At the same time, completely remove any side-shoots. In the second winter, choose three to five strong side-shoots that are growing at a wide, spreading angle to form permanent branches, and cut these back by between one-half (the more vigorous ones) and two-thirds (the less vigorous) to just above an outward-pointing bud. Remove all other side-shoots completely.

By the third winter, the branches will have grown strong new shoots. Choose between six and 10 of these to retain as a permanent framework, and cut them back

Only when mature apple trees are seriously congested with dead, diseased or crossing branches should they be pruned

by one half to two-thirds, cutting just above outward-pointing buds. At the same time cut back any side-shoots growing inside the framework to just above four buds from the base to encourage the development of spurs. Leave some laterals on the outside of the bush unpruned to form flower buds for 'renewal pruning', and remove any unwanted branches completely. This process can be repeated in the fourth winter, by which time the framework of the tree should be complete and no further pruning of leaders should be necessary.

Pruning for fruit production: continue with spur pruning (page 75) on the inside of the bush, and renewal pruning (page 76) on the outside.

STANDARD AND HALF-STANDARD TREES

Allow the maiden to grow on for at least a year after planting until it is well above the height at which the lowest permanent branch is required. For half-standards this is about 1.2m (4ft), for standards about 2m (6½ft). During this time, any laterals that develop should be cut back to 3-5cm (1¼-2in) from their bases in winter, and pinched back again to five leaves from their bases in summer. Their presence helps to strengthen the main stem, but they will be removed completely once the stem has reached the required height. The tree may then be pruned to produce an open centre, as I've described above.

DWARF PYRAMIDS

This shape was developed as a simple way of producing fruit intensively. The aim is to produce a tree about 2m (6½ft) high with a central stem from which branches about 45cm (18in) long grow out in tiers in a more or less pyramidal shape.

Once you gain confidence in formative pruning and training, you will derive satisfaction from trying some of the more spectacular styles such as the winged pyramid

Formative pruning: After planting a maiden on M 9 or M 26 rootstock, cut it back to a bud about 40cm (16in) from soil level. The following winter, cut back the central leader to leave about 20cm (8in) of new growth, cutting to above a bud pointing in the opposite direction to the last pruning (in order to keep the stem as straight as possible). At the same time, cut back all side branches to about 18cm (7in), to downward-pointing buds.

In mid- or late sumer of the following year, leave all the leading shoots unpruned, but cut back all laterals not required for the framework to three leaves, or about 10cm (4in), and all sub-laterals to one leaf beyond the basal cluster. Then in winter, again cut back the central leader to leave about 20cm (8in) of new growth, again cutting to a bud facing in the opposite direction to the last pruning, and cut back side branches again to leave about 18cm (7in) of new growth.

Continue summer and winter pruning in the same way for the third and subsequent years, until the tree reaches the required height. Then cut the central leader back to its base each year in late spring. Once the branches reach a total length of about 45cm (18in) they should be summer pruned to check further growth and encourage the development of fruiting spurs. Any thinning of branches or spurs that is necessary as the tree gets older should be done in winter.

Pruning neglected trees: I've described the pruning of neglected trees on page 10, but should add the following in relation to fruit trees. Always bear in mind that once you begin to prune an old tree, annual pruning will be needed for many years. Think carefully if you would be better leaving the old tree for its aesthetic appeal and planting new trees for fruit production.

Pears

Pears are generally less hardy than apples and slower to mature, but are pruned in exactly the same way. There is, however, less choice of rootstocks: 'Quince A' is moderately vigorous and 'Quince C' is slightly less vigorous, but both require good growing conditions. There are no dwarfing rootstocks; and a mature free-standing pear tree can take up a great deal of space. However, pears are very tolerant of training and pruning; and all of the methods used for apples may equally successfully be applied to pears. They thrive particularly well in restricted forms such as cordons or espaliers. In these cases the summer pruning is best done a week or so earlier than for apples.

ABOVE: Even a garden fence will provide satisfactory support for an espalier provided stong horizontal wires are attached to it

LEFT: A pear tree trained in espalier fashion against a wall is not only beautiful but offers the tree the benefit of warmth from the wall itself

Plums

66 *Once a free-standing plum tree is established and trained in a favourable site, it requires very little pruning. However, the blossom opens early and often suffers from frost damage, the fruit and buds are very susceptible to bird damage, and to disease, the wood tends to be brittle and may break under the weight of fruit, and the potentially lethal disease silver leaf is an ever-present threat. These risks can all be minimised by pruning in spring and summer (the spores of the silver-leaf fungus are present only in autumn and winter), by building up a strong framework of branches, and by training trees against walls for protection in cold areas.* 99

ROOTSTOCKS

Until recently, the only rootstocks available (principally 'Myrobalan B' and 'Brompton') were very vigorous. Now, however, other rootstocks have been developed, most importantly 'St Julien A' and the more dwarfing 'Pixy', and these should be chosen for all garden use. Nonetheless, don't expect that they will offer anything like the same degree of growth restriction as apple rootstocks.

Plums are usually trained as bushes, half-standards, compact pyramids or fans; and these forms are equally applicable to damsons, gages and bullaces. Always bear in mind, when pruning plums, that they bear their fruit on growth made during the previous year, and also on short spurs on older wood.

BUSHES AND HALF-STANDARDS

These are trained essentially like open-centred apple trees (page 80). For growing as a bush tree, the fruiting variety should be grafted on 'Pixy' rootstock, and as a half-standard, on 'St Julien A'. Both will need staking for at least the first four or five years.

Formative pruning: A maiden plum is best planted in late autumn, but should not be pruned until bud-break in early spring. Then cut back the leader to just above four or five plump buds at the required height, allowing for a stem of about 90cm (34in) for a bush and 1.4m (4½ft) for a half-standard. Any laterals should be cut back to about 7.5cm (13in). They will eventually be removed but, for the time being, help to strengthen the main stem.

Even on modern rootstocks, a mature free-standing plum tree will always be a large plant

A newly planted standard plum must have a stout stake, carefully tied with a belt-style tree tie

The following summer, pinch back any new growth on the laterals, leaving no more than four or five leaves. By early spring of the second year, several strong new shoots will have developed. Choose four that are well-spaced and wide-angled to form permanent branches. Cut each back by one-half to two-thirds to an outward-facing bud. Remove all laterals.

In the spring of the third year choose up to eight strong, outward-growing secondary branches to form a balanced framework. Cut the new growth on all of these back by between one-half and two-thirds, always cutting to just above outward-facing buds. At the same time, prune back laterals on the inside of the tree to about 10cm (4in), but leave laterals on the outside unpruned.

Pruning for fruit production: The main framework of branches is now in place. Generally it will be necessary only to shorten laterals on the inside of the tree to prevent it becoming

overcrowded. Any suckers that grow out of the rootstock should be removed promptly, and in spring any shoots stripped by birds should be cut back to a healthy bud.

PYRAMIDS

The aim is to create a cone-shaped tree on a central 2m (6½ft) high trunk. It will need staking for the first five years.

Formative pruning: Use either 'St Julien A' or 'Pixy' rootstock. Plant a feathered maiden in late autumn and start pruning at bud-break in spring. Cut back the stem to about 1.5m (5ft), remove completely any laterals from the bottom 50cm (20in) of the stem, and reduce the remaining ones by about half, cutting to just above downward-facing buds.

In midsummer of the following year, cut back the laterals growing directly from the stem to about 20cm (8in), and sub-laterals (shoots growing out of the laterals) to 15cm (6in). Leave the central leader unpruned.

At bud-break in spring of the second

Careful initial training is important for a pyramid plum tree but as it matures, relatively little maintenance pruning should be needed

year, cut back the new growth on the leader by two-thirds, to a bud pointing in the opposite direction to the last pruning. Continue to do this each spring until the leader reaches the required height. Subsequently, the new growth should be cut back to its base late each spring.

Pruning for fruit production: In midsummer of the second year, cut back the branch leaders to 20cm (8in) and laterals to 15cm (6in), again cutting to above downward-facing buds. This regime of summer pruning should be continued every year but cutting less each time until eventually the tree should 'settle down' and require very little pruning. At the same time, remove any over-vigorous shoots that will spoil the shape of the top of the tree, and any crossing or overcrowded laterals.

FANS

These may be grown either on 'St Julien A' rootstock, against a wall or fence about 2m (6½ft) high and 5m (16ft) long or on 'Pixy', when you will need a space of about 2 x 4m (6½ x 13ft).

Formative pruning: As peaches, see page 86.

Pruning for fruit production: In order to encourage the growth of new spurs, pinch back in summer any new shoots not needed for the framework to just above six or seven leaves from the base. After the fruit has been picked, shorten these shoots further by cutting them back to three leaves from the base. At the same time, cut out any old or unfruitful wood, and any very vigorous upright shoots.

In spring each year, remove any shoots growing directly towards or away from the wall or fence. Thin laterals if necessary so that they are about 10cm (4in) apart.

Cherries

❝ Sweet cherries and bitter cherries bear their fruit in different ways and, therefore, require different pruning methods. I find the sweet cherry a problematic plant, as it grows into a large tree, is slow to start cropping, birds tend to eat all of the fruit and it is very prone to blackfly infestation. Even on the growth-limiting rootstock 'Colt', a free-standing tree may grow to about 8m (25ft) in height. Older rootstocks can produce trees of 13m (42ft). The best solution for most gardeners is to fan-train sweet cherries, on a 'Colt' rootstock, so that they can be protected from birds by netting. This will require a wall span of about 3 x 5m (10 x 16ft), and a system of horizontal support wires. ❞

FANS

Formative pruning: An unfeathered maiden sweet cherry should be planted in late autumn but not pruned until early spring, when it should be cut back to a bud at a height of about 40cm (16in). Choose a bud which is pointing left or right, with another below it pointing in the opposite direction. As shoots grow out from these buds during the summer, tie them to canes placed at an angle of 45 degrees. Remove any other shoots at the same time.

In early spring of the second year, cut back the arms of the fan to buds about 30cm (12in) from the main stem. During this summer select four to six strong shoots growing out from the arms to

Most stone fruits are easily trained as fans; but the training must begin immediately after planting

form the 'ribs' of the fan: tie them to canes so they radiate outwards and are evenly spaced.

In early spring of the third year, cut back all leading shoots to a bud, leaving about 50cm (20in) of the previous year's growth. During the summer, select and tie in to canes three to six shoots

Fan training a Morello cherry makes netting against birds much easier to accomplish

growing out from each rib. Remove completely any further unwanted shoots, and shorten sub-lateral shoots to about 10cm (4in).

The fan should be complete by the fourth spring, but if not, selected leaders may be cut back to stimulate the growth of new shoots that can be trained in during the summer.

Pruning for fruit production: The formation of fruiting spurs is encouraged by restricting growth in summer. Pinch back sub-laterals to five or six leaves, or about 15cm (6in), and in early autumn shorten them again, cutting back to three buds, or about 10cm (4in). On mature trees it may be necessary to thin out the spurs, and this should be done in spring.

BUSHES AND TREES

If space is available, bush or standard trees may be grown and trained as for plums (see page 82), with formative pruning performed at bud-break in spring. Once the tree is established, all that is required is the removal of any damaged or crossing branches, which should be done in summer. The plants will need staking for the first four or five years.

BITTER CHERRIES

The bitter or Morello cooking cherry is less vigorous than the sweet cherry, and may be grown on the rootstock 'Colt' to make a bush tree, a central-leader pyramid or a fan. Almost all fruit is borne on the previous summer's growth.

BUSH TREES

The aim is to make a tree about 3m (10ft) high, in which young wood regularly replaces older wood that has already fruited. It will need staking for the first four or five years.

Formative pruning: Plant a feathered maiden in late autumn, but don't prune it until bud-break in spring. Cut back the central stem to a height of about 1m (3ft), just above four or five strong, well-placed laterals which will form the main branches. Shorten these laterals by about two-thirds, to outward-facing buds. Remove any laterals below them. Build up the head of the tree over the next two or three years by cutting back the previous summer's growth in early spring by one-half to two-thirds, mostly to outward-facing buds.

Pruning for fruit production: In order to encourage the development of young shoots, cut back about one-quarter of the fruited shoots after harvest to just above the emergence of a vigorous new shoot, which will bear fruit in the following year.

PYRAMID TREES

Grown on 'Colt' rootstock, these will be 2-3m (6½-10ft) high, and will require summer pruning to maintain their shape. They will need staking for the first five or six years.

Formative pruning: Form the pyramid as for a plum (see page 83).

Pruning for fruit production: In late summer of the third year, after the tree has borne its first crop, encourage the development of new shoots by cutting back shoots that have fruited to just above the emergence of a vigorous new shoot, which will bear fruit in the following year. Repeat this every summer to maintain a supply of new wood.

FANS

These will require a wall or fence of about 2 x 5m (6½ x 16ft), and a system of horizontal support wires.

Formative pruning: As for peaches on page 86.

Pruning for fruit production: In spring and early summer thin out the new shoots growing on the main framework of branches, so they are about 10-15cm (4-6in) apart. Tie in the retained shoots. Then in late summer, after the fruit has been picked from these shoots, cut them back to vigorous new shoots at their bases.

The self-fertile sweet cherry variety 'Stella' grown on the rootstock 'Colt' makes the most manageable garden tree

Peaches

❝ It's perfectly possible to grow peaches and nectarines in temperate areas if they are fan-trained against a wall. They are usually grown on the rootstock 'St Julien A'. Nonetheless, in many areas, including mine, peach leaf curl disease is an insurmountable problem and apricots are much more reliable alternatives. ❞

FANS

A wall space of about 2 x 5m (6½ x 16ft) will be required, with a system of horizontal support wires.

Formative pruning: Plant a feathered maiden in late autumn, but don't start pruning until early spring. Cut it back then to a lateral about 60cm (24in) high, just above two other strong laterals, facing in opposite directions, which will form the arms of the fan. Cut back all other laterals below these to one bud. Tie in the top lateral to grow vertically, then in midsummer cut back this top shoot completely. As the arms grow, tie them in to canes, to grow diagonally out from the stem.

In early spring of the second year cut back the arms to wood buds or triple buds (consisting of a wood bud and two flower buds) about 30-45cm (12-18in) from the stem. During the summer choose four shoots on each arm to form the 'ribs' of the fan, and tie them to canes. Pinch back all other shoots to one leaf.

After fruiting, the old fruited shoot should be cut out and a lower, replacement shoot, tied in to take its place

ABOVE: Peach and nectarine fruits are borne on lateral shoots

In early spring of the third year, cut back all leading stems of the ribs by about one-third, to just above downward-facing buds. Then in early summer, tie in new growth to fill in the fan. In late summer, pinch back to about 45cm (18in) any laterals not needed as ribs and tie them in. The tree will begin to bear fruit in the fourth year on these shoots, which should be about 10-15cm (4-6in) apart. Pinch back any unwanted laterals to one leaf.

In the winter of the third year, lightly prune all leading shoots, removing about one-quarter of new growth. In the fourth and subsequent years, if new growth is needed to fill out the fan, continue to prune all leading shoots by one-quarter in winter. When the fan has filled the available space, stop the growth of the outermost shoots by pinching out the tips in summer.

Pruning for fruit production: It's important every year to replace laterals that have borne fruit with new shoots. Each lateral that is going to bear fruit produces side-shoots along its length. In spring choose two of these leafy side-shoot buds near the base, one to be a replacement lateral and one to be a reserve, and allow them to grow. Any other side-shoots are unwanted and their leafy buds should be pinched out. In early summer, when the fruiting laterals reach 45cm (18in) in length, pinch back the tips. After the fruit has been picked, cut back the laterals that have fruited to just above the replacement laterals or, if any of these are weak or damaged, to the reserves, and tie them in.

In order to obtain fruit of a good size it may be necessary to thin out. This should be done in two stages, in early summer and in midsummer, leaving the peaches to grow about 25cm (10in) apart. Every spring, cut out any shoots growing directly towards or away from the wall.

Nectarines

❝ *Nectarines are smooth-skinned varieties of peach, and, I think, have an even more delicious flavour. They are cultivated in the same way as peaches, except that the individual fruit may be allowed to grow slightly closer together, about 15cm (6in), instead of 20cm (8in).* ❞

Apricots

❝ *Apricots are hardier than peaches although they blossom earlier. They may be grown free-standing but much the best way is fan-trained against a warm, sunny wall where they can be covered with protective plastic or mesh screens once the blossom opens. In my rather cold garden, they crop very successfully in this way. They are usually grown on 'St Julien A' rootstock.* ❞

FANS

Formative pruning: As for peaches, see page 86.

Pruning for fruit production: Most fruit is borne on short spurs on two- or three-year-old wood. In order to encourage the growth of these spurs, pinch out the tips of new shoots in late spring or early summer. In spring, remove any shoots growing directly towards or away from the wall. Old wood will eventually become unproductive, so every two or three years in late summer remove a proportion of older side-shoots that have fruited.

Apricots are easily trained as fans and make good free-standing trees

Figs

" *Although figs are hardy, they will only reliably produce fruit in cool climates if grown in a warm, sheltered position. They thrive best if fan-trained against a warm, sunny wall.* "

FANS

A fan-trained fig will require a space of about 3 x 5m (10 x 16ft), and a system of horizontal support wires as well as canes arranged in a fan shape in the early stages.

Formative pruning: As for peaches, see page 86.

Pruning for fruit production: In Britain and other cooler areas, fig fruit will not reach harvesting size within one season. The important fruits are the pea-sized ones that appear in late summer at the tips of young shoots. If they survive the winter they should ripen by late summer or early autumn the following year. A second crop develops on new shoots in spring but fails to ripen, and should be removed in late autumn.

In early summer, pinch back to about five leaves from the base all of the young shoots growing out of the ribs of the fan. These shoots will harden and produce embryo fruits in late summer. In midsummer, some old and unfruitful wood may be thinned out to let in more sunlight to ripen the fruit.

I find it best to do the bulk of the pruning in spring, leaving on the old wood to give protection in the winter. So, in spring, cut back to 2.5cm (1in) about half of the shoots that have borne fruit, in order to encourage new growth. The shoots that remain should be about 25-30cm (10-12in) apart, and should be tied in. Any other unwanted shoots should be removed completely and you should remove any shoots growing directly towards or away from the wall. If a whole branch of a mature fan-trained fig becomes unfruitful it, too, should be cut out in early spring and a strong new shoot from near the base trained in as a replacement.

Walnut trees eventually become very large and are plants for big gardens only

Walnuts

" *The English Walnut,* Juglans regia *and the Black Walnut,* J. nigra *are slow-growing, but eventually huge trees. If unpruned they may grow to 8 x 4m (25 x 13ft) after 20 years, and reach 30 x 15m (100 x 50ft) at maturity. They are generally grown as standards but will not normally bear fruit for the first 10 or 15 years. If space is available, however, they make magnificent flowering trees with, ultimately, a delicious crop. The trees offered for sale are very rarely named, but it's important to obtain grafted plants whose scion wood comes from a parent tree that fruits freely.* "

Figs are big, vigorous plants, and are most conveniently grown as fans

Pruning: After planting in late autumn, the young tree will need staking for the first year or two. The shoots bearing male flowers, which appear as drooping catkins, should be left unpruned, but all other shoot tips should be continually pinched back to about six leaves, two or three times each summer. With this method, the tree should start fruiting within 10 years, and will remain a manageable size. Don't attempt to prune mature trees, unless it is necessary to remove damaged or crowded branches. This should be done in late summer, as the tree will ooze sap ('bleed') heavily at other times.

Cobnuts and Filberts

❝ The cobnut or hazelnut, Corylus avellana, *and the filbert,* C. maxima, *make attractive small trees or large shrubs. They bear male and female flowers on the same tree, the males in catkins, the females inconspicuously. Their nuts are borne in autumn on light twiggy shoots. They can be grown as open-centred bushes, about 2m (6¹⁄₂ft) high, on stems of about 45cm (18in), or as trees reaching about 6 x 4m (20 x 13ft). All are self-fertile, but as the male and female flowers do not always open at the same time it makes sense to plant more than one variety. ❞*

Formative pruning: After planting a one-year-old tree in late autumn, cut back the leader to the desired height and remove any shoots from the stem. Four or five strong, evenly spaced shoots should at first be encouraged to develop from the head. For four to six years after planting, prune the bush or tree in winter, cutting the leaders back by about half

each time to an outward-facing bud. This will produce an open-centred head with eight to 10 branches. Any vigorous side-shoots should be cut back to three or four buds.

Pruning for fruit production: Nuts should start to appear four to six years after planting. The plants should then be pruned by 'brutting' in late summer: break by hand all strong side-shoots growing from the main branches and leave them hanging in order not to stimulate new growth. The broken shoots are then cut back to 5-8cm (2-3¹⁄₂in) in late winter or early spring.

Also in late winter or early spring, remove any dead or damaged wood, and cut back vigorous side-shoots to three or four buds. Do not prune the twiggy shoots that bear the tiny red female flowers, but it is beneficial if the male catkins are buffeted by this pruning operation, as it helps to distribute their pollen.

Any suckers that appear at the base of the trees should be twisted and pulled out.

Filberts produce large numbers of nuts but for optimum production, careful pruning is needed

CLIMBING FRUIT

Grapevine

" *Outdoor grapevines thrive best against a sunny, sheltered wall, and require a support system of sturdy horizontal wires spaced about 30cm (12in) apart. Greenhouse vines are also best when in a sunny, sheltered position; lean-to greenhouses, being warmer, are preferable. There are many different methods of pruning grapevines, but the one I describe here works well for me and is both simple and effective.* "

Pruning an outdoor vine: Immediately after planting in early winter, cut the main stem down to about 60-75cm (24-30in) above soil level, cutting to just above a bud. Support the stem, or 'rod', by tying it to a vertical cane. During the first summer, allow it to grow up to the topmost wire, and then pinch out its top. The strongest of the side-shoots should be tied in to the wires on either side of the rod, and pinched out just beyond five leaves from their base. Any other side-shoots should be pinched out altogether.

In the winter a year after planting, cut back the rod by about half, and cut back the side-shoots to about 2.5-5cm (1-2in) from their bases. During the second summer new side-shoots will grow out from these stubs: only one strong one should be allowed to develop and tied in to the support wires; weaker ones should be pinched out. In winter two years after planting, again cut back the rod, which will gradually, nevertheless, be approaching the top of the wall, and cut back the side-shoots to leave 2.5-5cm (1-2in) stubs.

The vine should start to bear flowers and fruit during the following summer, but not too many should be allowed to develop while the plant is young; only about one per lateral in the first fruiting year, two in the second and three in later years. To ensure this, pinch out the laterals in summer just beyond three leaves after the first flower cluster in the first year, the second in the second year, and the third thereafter.

Every winter, the side-shoots should be cut back to leave short stubs; and when the rod has reached the top of the wires it should be treated like a side-shoot and cut back to the same point each year.

The grapes should be thinned out when they are about 5mm (¼in) in diameter. Use blunt-ended scissors and remove about half of each bunch, so the remaining fruits will grow larger.

Pruning a greenhouse vine:
The vine should be planted just outside the greenhouse, and the stem passed through a hole in the wall close to soil level. From then on, the training and pruning is essentially the same as for an outdoor vine.

In a lean-to greenhouse, the rod should be trained up the side wall and along the angle between the lower end of the roof and the wall, with the side-shoots trained up the slope of the roof. In a free-standing house, the rod should be trained up the end wall, and pinched out when it reaches the top so that it branches. Each branch is then trained along the angle between the lower edges of the roof and the side walls, with the side-shoots trained up the slope of the roof on either side to meet at the ridge.

LEFT: Free-standing grapevines outdoors must be trained against horizontal wires

BELOW: Excess growth on grapevines is most simply pinched out with finger and thumb

Kiwi fruit

Actinidia deliciosa (syn. chinensis), the Chinese gooseberry, requires similar growing conditions to a grapevine, preferably a sheltered, sunny wall, and it is pruned in a similar way. It will require a sturdy support system of horizontal wires spaced about 45cm (18in) apart, up to a height of 2m (6½ft). Alternatively, in very mild areas, it can be trained against free-standing wires. I haven't described this system here, but the method of erecting the support wires and the subsequent pruning will be found in Best Soft Fruit.

Most varieties are unisexual, and so you will need to plant a male and female together. If space is limited (and they are very vigorous plants) they may be put in the same planting hole, and the shoots then trained in opposite directions. Nurseries, indeed, commonly sell two plants in the same pot. One self-fertile variety is available, 'Blake', but it is early flowering and bears a smaller quantity of smaller fruit.

Pruning against a wall: After planting in early autumn or, preferably, in mid-spring, cut back the main stem to just above the lowest wire, and tie it in to the wire. As new shoots develop, tie one to grow vertically and two horizontally along the wires, and cut out any others. As the main central shoot grows upwards, tie it to the next wire and train in two more horizontal shoots.

Repeat this process until the central shoot reaches the top wire, which it should do within two years.

When the side-shoots are about 1m (3ft) long, pinch out their tips to encourage sub-laterals to grow, and these should then be pinched out in summer just above five leaves from the base. By the third year, some of these sub-laterals will bear fruit and become fruiting spurs. They should be pinched out at five leaves beyond the fruit cluster in early summer. Those that do not bear fruit should be pinched out just beyond five leaves above the base.

In winter, all of the sub-laterals should be cut back, either to two buds beyond where the fruit developed, if they bore fruit, or to two buds from the base, if they did not. This process of pinching out and cutting back the fruiting shoots is then repeated every year.

Kiwi fruits are extremely vigorous and must be pruned and tied in carefully if they are not to get out of hand

HERBACEOUS PLANTS

❝The notion of pruning herbaceous plants will strike some gardeners as a bit odd. Nonetheless, bearing in mind that pruning is the removal of unwanted shoots and the manipulation of others to produce more attractive or productive plants, there is no reason to exclude them. I have given notes here on when to cut and when not to cut the main groups of herbaceous perennials. ❞

Most herbaceous plants should have dead flowerheads removed during the growing season, immediately after flowering. This will not only make them look tidier, and encourage new growth, but in some cases, for example with many of the hardy geraniums, *Nepeta* and *Omphalodes*, it will encourage a second flowering. However, the dead flower-heads of some plants remain attractive, such as *Sedum spectabile*, *Astilbe*, and *Astrantia*; and others, such as poppies, hostas, and perennial honesty, have especially attractive seedheads, in which case (unless they are required for flower arrangements), it makes sense to leave them standing. They become particularly appealing when covered with winter frost and snow.

It's important also to bear in mind that seedheads left on over winter will provide invaluable winter food for birds. The presence of small flocks of finches and other seed-eating birds is itself appealing enough, but remember too that they may also thereby be distracted from feeding on your fruit buds.

In general, any foliage that becomes damaged, discoloured or diseased during the growing season should be carefully removed at once, before the disease has a chance to spread. Hollyhocks, for example, are very prone to rust, which attacks the lower leaves first. These should be collected and destroyed before the spores are spread to the upper foliage.

In winter, most herbaceous plants die down completely, leaving only a mass of dead stems above soil level. In general, the only pruning that is required is to cut these down and use them, preferably shredded, to make compost. This can be done in the autumn for most hardy varieties; but in areas where there are very cold winters, and for less hardy plants such as *Acanthus*, *Kniphofia*, *Romneya* and *Verbascum*, the foliage

An attractive herbaceous border does not happen by accident but needs careful tying and some selective pruning

should be left until the spring, to give the plants some protection against frost.

Some herbaceous plants such as *Epimedium, Omphalodes, Polygonum affine, Pulmonaria* and *Stachys byzantina* have perfectly hardy evergreen or semi-evergreen leaves, and in these cases only dead or discoloured leaves need to be removed.

A few herbaceous plants, notably *Aconitum* and *Delphinium*, benefit from having some of the stems and also some of the flower spikes thinned out in spring in order to encourage bigger, stronger blooms. Leave about five or six of the strongest spikes to grow on each plant. On dahlias and chrysanthemums, when large flowers are required for cutting or exhibition, selective thinning out of the

ABOVE: Although some plants from this autumn border, like the dahlias, will be lifted completely, others will simply have top growth cut back while others can be left for birds to feed on the seed heads in the winter

RIGHT: When cutting out dead stems, be sure to prune back to soil level

buds and side-shoots is required. On dahlias, simple removal of a few side-shoots is generally adequate but with chrysanthemums, the procedure, generally called stopping, is more complicated and varies with the variety and type of chrysanthemum, so specialist guidance should be sought if you grow any other than garden 'spray' varieties.

INDEX

Abies 30
Abies balsamea f. hudsonia 30
Abies concolor 'Compacta' 30
Abies grandis 30
Abies koreana 30
Abies veitchii 30
Abutilon 30
Abutilon vitifolium 30
Acanthus 92
Acer 15, 30
  'Dissectum' 30
Acer cappadocicum 30
Acer griseum 30
Acer japonicum 30
Acer negundo 30
Acer palmatum 30
Acer platanoides 30
Acer pseudoplatanus
  'Brilliantissimum' 30
Acer rubrum 30
Acer saccharinum 30
Acer shirasawanum 'Aureum' 30
acid-soil fruits 74, 74
Aconitum 93
Actinidia 30
Actinidia deliciosa syn. chinensis
  91, 91
  'Blake' 91
Actinidia kolomikta 30, 30
Akebia 30
Akebia quinata 30
Alexandrian laural see Danae
alpine plants 42
Amelanchier 30
Amelanchier canadensis 30, 31
Amelanchier larmarkii 30, 31
Ampelopsis 30
Ampelopsis glandulos var.
  brevipedunculata 30
anvil secateurs 8, 20
apical dominance 5, 13
apple trees 10, 11, 14-15, 24,
  25, 28, 75-7, 76-7, 80-81,
  80
  rootstocks 75
  staking 75
apricots 87, 87
Araucaria 31
Araucaria araucana 31, 31
Arbutus 31
Arctostaphylos 31
Arctostaphylos nevadensis 31
Arctostaphylos uva-ursi 31
Aristolochia 31
Aristolochia durior 31
aromatic hedges 64, 65
Artemisia 31
Artemisia abrotanum 31
ash trees 10
Astilbe 92
Astrantia 92
Atriplex 32
Atriplex halimus 32
Aucuba 32
autumn pruning 25, 28, 56-7,
  71, 79, 92
Azalea 50-51

Ballerina fruit trees 76
basal collars 14, 25, 25, 30

batters 63, 63
Bay laurel 67
Beech see Fagus
Berberis 32
Berberis darwinii 32, 32
Berberis julianae 32
Berberis lologensis 32
Berberis x stenophylla 32, 65
Berberis thunbergii 32, 65
Betula 32
Betula pendula 'Youngii' 32
Bignonia 32
Birch see Betula
bird damage 82, 84, 84, 92
bird food 92, 93
bitter cherries 84-5, 84
Bittersweet see Celastrus
Black Walnut see Juglans nigra
blackberry 71, 71
  hybrids 71
blackcurrant 72, 72
  'Ben Sarek' 72
blackfly infestation 84
Blackthorn see Prunus spinosa
bleeding 89
blueberry 74, 74
  'Blue Crop' 74
Bottlebrush see Callistemon
Box see Buxus
branches 4, 6, 6, 72
  bending 5, 13
  broken 6, 14
  lateral 6, 6, 24, 28, 28-9, 75,
    76, 80, 83
  removal of 10, 11, 13, 14-15,
    14-5, 24,
    24, 25
  sap drawers 11
  sub-laterals 6, 6
  weak 6, 6
Bridal Wreath see Spiraea
  nipponica
broken branches 6
Broom see Cytisus, Genista
brutting 89
Buddleja 32-3
Buddleja alternifolia 16, 21, 22,
  32
Buddleja davidii 17, 32, 32
Buddleja globosa 32
buds 16, 18
  apical dominance 5, 13
  flower 75-6
  lateral 7
  strong 7, 13
  terminal 6, 7
  weak 7
Bush honeysuckle see Diervilla
Bush Roses 56, 65
bush shapes 24, 24, 75, 82, 84
Butcher's broom see Ruscus
Butterfly bush see Buddleja
Buxus 33, 62, 65, 67, 67, 68
Buxus microphylla 33
Buxus sempervirens 33, 63
  'Suffruticosa' 33
by-pass secateurs see scissor
  secateurs

Calico bush see Kalmia
Callistemon 33
Calluna 33
Camellia 16, 33
Campsis 33, 33
Campsis grandiflora 33
Campsis radicans 33
canes 70, 71, 71

cankers 14, 14, 57
Caragana 33
Caragana arborescens 33
Carpenteria californica 34
Carpinus betulus 62, 64, 65
Caryopteris 34
Catalpa 34
Catalpa bignonioides 34
Ceanothus 34
  'Cynthia Postan' 34
  'Perle Rose' 34
Cedar see Cedrus
Cedrus 34
Cedrus deodara 'Aurea' 34
Celastrus 34
Celastrus orbiculatus 34
Celastrus scandens 34
centres
  crowded 7, 7
  open 7, 7, 80-81, 80, 82
Ceratostigma 34
Ceratostigma griffithii 34
Ceratostigma willmottianum 34
Cercis 35
Chaenomeles 35
chain saws 9
Chamaecyparis 35
Chamaecyparis lawsoniana
  'Ellwoodii' 35
  'Ellwood's Gold' 35
  'Minima Aurea' 35
  'Minima Glauca' 35
Chamaecyparis pisifera
  'Boulevard' 35
cherry trees 84-5, 84-5
  'Colt' 84, 85
chestnuts 24
Chilean bellflower see
  Lapageria rosea
Chinese gooseberry see
  Actinidia deliciosa
Chocolate vine see Akebia
Chiosya 36
  'Sundance' 36
Choisya ternata 36
chrysanthemums 17, 93
Clematis 16, 26-7, 26-7, 35
  'Jackmanii' 35
Clematis alpina 35
Clematis florida 35
Clematis lanuginosa 35
Clematis macropetala 35
Clematis montana 35, 35
Clematis patens 35
Clematis tangutica 35
Clematis viticella 35
climbing fruit 90-91, 90-91
Climbing honeysuckle see
  Lonicera
climbing plants 12-13, 13, 26-7,
  26-7, 30-55
Climbing Roses 4, 5, 59-60
Cobnut see Corylus avellana
Columnar fruit trees 76
conifer hedges 62
container plants 74, 75
coppicing 24
coral spot 15, 15
cordon fruit trees 4, 27, 27,
  72-3, 72, 73, 75, 76-7, 77,
  81
Cornus 22, 36
Cornus alba 36
Cornus canadensis 36
Cornus florida 36
Cornus kousa 36
Cornus mas 36

Cornus stolonifera 36
  'Flaviramea' 36
Corylus 36, 64
Corylus avellana 36, 89
  'Contorta' 36
Corylus maxima 98, 89
  'Purpurea 36, 89
Cotoneaster 36
  'Cornubia' 36
Cotoneaster conspicuus 36
Cotoneaster horizontalis 36
Cotoneaster microphyllus 36
Cotoneaster salicifolius 36
  'Rothschildianus' 36, 37
Cotoneaster simonsii 65
Cotton lavender see Santolina
Crab apple see Malus
cranberry 74, 74
  'C.N.' 74
  'Franklin' 74
Crataegus 36, 62, 63, 67
Crataegus monogyna 36
Crinodendron 37
Crinodendron hookerianum 37
Cross vine see Bignonia
crotch 6
crowded centres 7, 7
crowns
  of trees 10, 13
Cupressus sp. 37, 62, 67
Cupressus arizonica 37
Cupressus x Cupressocyparis 37
Cupressus x Cupressocyparis
  leylandi 37, 65
Cupressus macrocarpa 37
Cypress see Cupressus sp.
Cytisus 37
Cytisus battandieri 37
Cytisus x kewensis 37
Cytisus x praecox 'Allgold' 37

dahlias 17, 93, 93
damage control 14-15, 57, 82,
  92
damson trees 82
Danae 37
Daphne 37
Daphne odora 37
Daphne tangutica 37
deadheading 4, 19, 19, 21, 50,
  56, 57, 60-61, 92
Decumaria 37
Delphinium 93
Desfontainea spinosa 38
Deutzia 65
Deutzia x magnifica 12
diagonal cordons 76, 77
die-back 57
Diervilla 38
Diervilla sessilifolia 38
disease control 14-15, 14-15,
  17, 57, 82, 92
diseases 14-15, 14-15
  black spot 14-15, 57
  blackfly infestation 84
  cankers 14, 14, 57
  coral spot 15, 15
  fungi 14-15
  mildew 14, 15
  peach leaf curl 86
  rust 92
  silver leaf 10, 16, 17, 17, 82
Dogwood see Cornus
Douglas fir see Pseudotsuga
Drimys 38
Drimys winteri 38

'Dublin Bay' rose 4
Dutchman's pipe see Aristolochia
dwarf hedges 64
drawf pyramid trees 80, 80
dwarfing rootstocks 75, 75, 82

Elaeagnus 38
Elaeagnus pungens 'Maculata' 38,
  38
Elder see Sambucus
English Walnut see Juglans regia
Enkianthus 38
Enkianthus campanulatus 38
Enkianthus cernuus 38
Enkianthus perulatus 38
Epimedium 93
Erica 38
Erica carnea 38
  'Aurea' 38
Erica cinerea 38
Erica x darleyensis 38
Escallonia 38, 63
espalier fruit trees 27, 27, 75,
  77, 78-9, 78-9, 81, 81
Eucalyptus 38
Eucalyptus gunii divaricata 39
Eucryphia 39
Eucryphia x nymansensis
  'Nymansay' 39
Euonymus 39
Euonymus alatus 39
Euonymus europaeus 39
Euonymus fortunei 39

Fagus 39, 62, 63, 65
Fagus sylvatica 64
  Pendula 39
Fallopia 39
Fallopia baldschuanica 39
fan-trained fruit trees 4, 27, 28,
  71, 73, 75, 82, 83, 84, 84,
  85, 86-7, 87, 88, 88
Fatsia japonica 40
Fatsia japonica 40
x Fatshedera lizei 40
Fatsia lizei 40
feathering 75
  unfeathered maidens 77, 84
Ficus 41
Ficus pumila 41
fig trees 88-9, 88
Filbert see Corylus maxima
Firethorn see Pyracantha
Floribunda Roses 19 58
  'Beautiful Britain' 59
flower buds 75-6
flower clusters 19
flowering times 16-17, 20-23
flowers 13, 16
foliage plants 13
  variegated 13
Forsythia 16, 40, 64
Forsythia x intermedia 40
  'Lynwood' 40
  'Spectabilis' 40
Forsythia suspensa 40
Fothergilla 40
Fothergilla major 40
Fraxinus 40
Fraxinus excelsior 40
  'Pendula' 40
Fraxinus ornus 40
Fremontodendron 40, 41
  'Californian Glory' 40
fruit 17, 17
fruit production 77, 80, 83, 84,
  85, 87, 88, 89, 89